The Fiction Writer's Sexuality Guide:

Sex—It's More Than a Scene

The Fiction Writer's Sexuality Guide:

Sex—It's More Than a Scene

Dr. J. | Donna Jennings, Ph.D.

Passion Works Press LLC

Published in the United States

By Passion Works Press LLC

PO Box 219 Fernandina Beach, FL 32035

First Edition May 2024

10 9 8 7 6 5 4 3 2 1

Cover design and formatting: M. C. Miller

Editing: Kaitlin Schmidt, Arielle Haughee

Worksheet Graphics: Kaitlin Schmidt

Paperback: ISBN: 978-1-7338426-4-8

E-book: ISBN: 978-1-7338426-2-4

Printed in the U.S.A.

Also by Dr. J. | Donna Jennings

Purple Sex and Love Beyond Your Dreams: A Women's Guided Journal to Explore Your Sexual Self.

Chemical [se]X 2: Just One More

Contributor:

Sexy Strangers

The Big Book of Orgasms Vol 2

Best Bondage Erotica Vol 2

Rule 34 Vol 2

The Sexy Librarian's Dirty 30 Vol 3

The Big Book of Submission Vol 2

Best Women's Erotica of the Year, Vol 3

Shadows & Silhouettes (Cards of Passion Book Series) 8-8-2024

With Featured Authors for the Series

Danika Bloom: https://www.danikabloom.com/

Gabbi Black: https://gabbiblack.com/

Mischa Eliot: https://www.mischaeliot.com/

Sri Savita: https://sri-savita.com/

Ally Daine: https://allydaine.com/

Henrietta Holland: https://www.instagram.com/henriettaholland2024/

Kaitlin Schmidt: https://www.kaitlin-schmidt.com/

F. Leonora Solomon: https://fdotleonora.com/

Katia Hunter: https://badredheadmedia.com/

Praise for The Fiction Writer's Guide to Sexuality

"The Fiction Writer's Sexuality Guide demystifies the art of integrating sexuality into our stories, offering a new paradigm to enrich character depth and the reader connection to our characters and stories."

Danika Bloom, USA Today Best-Selling Romance Author

"Dr. J. walks readers through the art of crafting fully developed scenes that honor the power of sexual desire and make your stories realistic and captivating."

Rachel Kramer Bussel, author of *How to Write Erotica* and *Lap Dance Lust*

"For romance and erotica writers, as well as anyone studying craft and character development, *The Fiction Writer's Sexuality Guide* will help give a better handle on the who, what, why, and how-to of sex and sexuality in narrative."

Rebecca Brooks, Author of Wrong Man, Right Roommate

"Whether you're struggling to write your first "scene with sex" or you're an experienced author looking to diversify your fictional intimate moments and/or overcome sexual biases to add more to your writing toolbox, this book is for you."

Elle Ire, Goldie Award-winning author of Sapphic Speculative Romance.

"At last! A writing guide that regards sexuality as an essential part of any character in fiction. Packed with advice, relatable anecdotes and practical exercises to help writers engage with erotic scenes, this book is not just about writing scenes with sex well, it's about writing great fully rounded authentic characters."

Tabitha Rayne, Best Erotic Author-ETO Awards Editor-Frolic Me Magazine

"This is a very smart book that uses very practical examples to help authors build our writing skills. I particularly enjoyed the 5 Cs exercises and the information about describing body parts!"

Lainey Davis, USA Today Bestselling Author

"This is hands down the best resource I've come across for writing scenes with sex! Dr. J. breaks down sexuality in easy-to-understand perspectives that you can apply not only to your writing but also to your life."

Casey Harris-Parks, Founder and Editor at Heart Full of Ink

"I enjoyed how Dr. J. clearly explained, well, everything. As a writer who has been an award finalist for erotic romance, and who has written for erotic anthologies, I appreciate the straightforward, clear discussion of not only the mechanics of how to set up a scene involving sex, but also how to bring intimacy and meaning to those scenes. It's a book I wish I had when I first started writing."

Tamara Lush, Romance Novelist

"Dr. J.'s *The Fiction Writer's Sexuality Guide: Sex—It's More Than a Scene* is the writing gift that keeps on giving. It's a powerhouse of help on every page. Who would have thought a nonfiction guide would be a page-turner?

Perfect for any writer and author who writes romance, women's history, cozy mysteries, or erotica. It sets the what, the why, and the how for scene creation woven with the depth of sensitivity and sensuality."

Judith Briles, author of *The Authors Walk* and *How to Avoid Book Publishing Blunders*

"An instant classic to be added to any writer's toolbox! This is a must-read guide that demystifies the process of building characters of sexuality and nuance. It's a clever, step-by-step handbook that provides a top-notch, practical exploration of the creative process while supporting and encouraging the pioneering of self."

Rose Caraway, Host of *The Kiss Me Quick's* Erotica Podcast

"Whoa! Get ready to be transformed. You will learn more about yourself than how to write about your characters and sex. Dr. J. writes with knowledge and expertise in both the sexuality and fiction writing fields. She peppers it with great resources and examples. The coupling of how to write a great sex story and how to incorporate the concepts of sex therapy are intertwined. Get ready for your own fantastic sex life and story!"

Joan C Sughrue, Med, BSN, RN
AASECT Certified Diplomate of Sex Therapy, AASECT Certified Supervisor

For Darryl, Heather, Mischa, and Maggie

and for all writers

looking to connect the meaning of sex

within their stories, through their characters, even if you didn't know it.

"Nothing you write will matter unless it moves the human heart." A.D. Hope.

Acknowledgments

Creating a book takes a team effort. My appreciation and heartfelt thanks go to my team.

At the percolation phase, The Florida Writers Association, who asked me to present my ideas about writing sex, Darryl Bollinger, who pushed me to get this book created, and John Grisham, who provided a little grist for my clarifications.

Heather Whitaker, my novel writing teacher, mentor, and friend.

Arielle Haughee of Orange Blossom Publishing provided the first edit.

Kaitlin Schmidt edited and polished my words. Her stellar insights of where I was going helped to make the entire manuscript cohesive. She is also the incredible designer of the Worksheets, and after reading my words, translated them into graphic art for you.

My Passion Works Author Group, who worked the chapters in real time, so I knew what would stick.

Danika Bloom who embraced my ideas and shared them with her Author Ever After Romance Community. She inspired me, (or pushed like Darryl) to make this content a course for the INFOSTACK Romance Writer's bundle for 2023.

Mischa Eliot, who always believed in me and worked beside me, as best friends do.

Frank and Bren, who support me every day with infinite love.

Table of Contents

Worksheets

Overview

The Fiction Writer's Sexuality Guide: Sex—It's More Than a Scene is a writing guidebook, written by a sex therapist and sexuality educator. The book provides authors with a template to write about sexuality in story and scene with confidence.

Highlights of Dr. J.'s Sex-Writing Paradigm

Introducing: A new paradigm for thinking about sexuality as a writer. Here are the highlights.

The Thread of Sex

Let's anchor sex in your story's first chapter. You are a story weaver, so when you set your writing frame, you must have the thread of sex tied and ready to pick up as your story moves. Don't think of sex as something you pull down from the shelf on an as-needed basis. If you know the character's sexuality exists at a macro level throughout the story, you can use it to create a richer character at the micro level of each individual scene.

Sex-Positive Framing

I use the phrase "scene with sex" instead of "sex scene." I invite you to do so as well. This moves you away from an automatic heteronormative stance. According to *Oxford University Press* (n.d.), "heteronormative" is defined as "denoting or relating to a world view that promotes heterosexuality as the normal or preferred sexual orientation." If you believe that "sex scene" means only penis-in-vagina (PinV) intercourse, then the words "scenes with sex" go beyond that and provides a place in your writer brain where you can incorporate diverse character information—love, relationships, sexual activities, and all types of sexual energy exchanges. With the new range of sex available, your characters will engage in physical activities based on your story specifically (the story arc, the character arc, a subplot sexual journey) in ways that serve your intentions for character development. You won't be writing the same old scenes with sex if you write them based on your character. How one "does" sex is as unique as a fingerprint. While scenes with sex are often structured the same way, one sex event is never like another.

You

The Person of the Writer: Embrace your teaching status. Write about sexuality with an eye for being fictionally realistic and factually accurate. Yes, I know you didn't take up teaching when you set out to write a story, but writing teaches. As a sex educator and sex therapist, I asked students and clients how they learned about sex, and reading novels was a frequent answer. So, I invite you to write with intention, starting by eliminating author intrusion.

Sex History

Build a sexual history for your character. It informs their sexual enjoyment and conflicts. These layers add rich information for wants, needs, and motivations when you require it. A sexual event of a character's past is a pivotal data point of their sexual makeup in the present, so each event provides specific information about the character.

PEMS Sexual Intimacy Model

PEMS stands for the **P**hysical, **E**motional, **M**ental, and **S**piritual components of the holistic person. Use this model in conjunction with the character's sex history for rich character development.

Scene-with-Sex Structure

Incorporate the spine of character connection by using the 5 Cs of Scene, and then refine the scene using four concepts: meaning of sex, pacing, sensual language, and emotional beats.

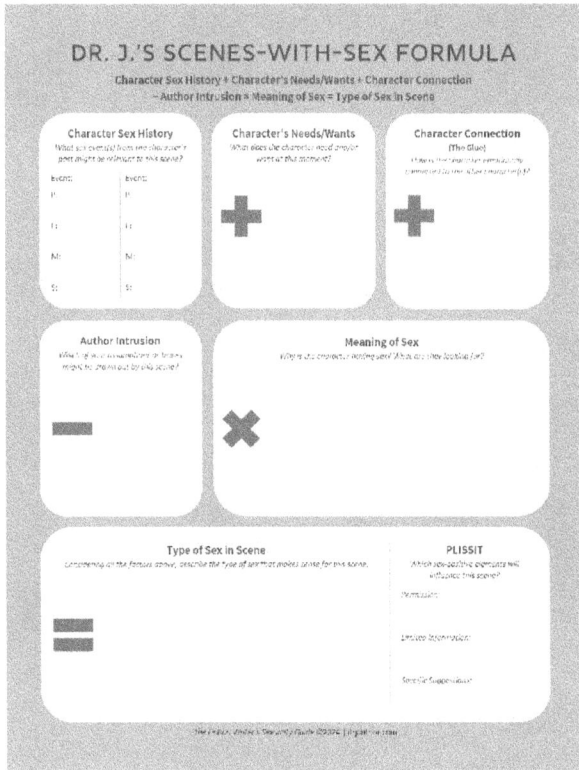

Dr. J.'s Scenes-with-Sex Formula Worksheet is available for you to plug information in as you are working with each element of the book. It serves to keep your new sexuality thinking perspective in the forefront as you write. A full set of worksheets is at the back of the book. With them, you will find a link to download fillable PDFs.

Within the book is a completed Scenes-with-Sex Formula worksheet example of a story showcased within the book.

Sign up below for **Dr. J.'s Newsletter** to keep up with the latest events, releases, and sales.

Link: https://qr1.be/ZI1B

Navigating This Book

Five icons are used throughout this book to indicate the following types of content:

The **book** icon precedes personal anecdotes.

The **question mark** icon precedes self-reflection questions.

The **toolbox** icon precedes concrete writing strategies.

The **data** icon precedes examples of how to apply a strategy.

The **writing** icon precedes opportunities to practice or engage with a strategy.

When a key term or concept is explored or defined for the first time, it is written in bold, like so:

Management of Self in sex is about establishing clarity in where your personal boundaries stop and start. Think of it as a circle around you, at arm's length: Everything inside the circle is you and your Self. Everything outside the circle is not you.

Initial Intake

Hello and welcome to the book, which I hope will alter how you think and write about sexuality within the context of storytelling. This guide is for you, whether you are interested in creating scenes with sex or want to weave sexuality seamlessly throughout all your writing.

My name is Dr. J., and I am excited to offer you my knowledge and experience. I am a retired sex therapist, sexuality consultant, and sex educator. Since 2016, I have been taking my academic learning along with my professional experience and moving into a new sexuality niche: writing erotica and erotic romance.

Now, I'm sharing what I've learned with all fiction writers. With this guide, I offer you a detailed new paradigm about sex.

The Sexuality Problems Writers Face

To start, have you thought or said any of these things pertaining to writing about sexuality?

- *When I'm writing, I skip the sex scene and write: Insert sex here.*

- *I'm told that sex sells, so I should put sex into my story?*

- *I'm scared to write about sex. It makes me nervous.*

- *I don't want to address sex. I'll do it wrong.*

- *I should know how to write it, right? It's part of the human experience.*

- *I don't have a clue how to write sex scenes.*

- *I'm uncomfortable talking or writing about sex. I don't have the language.*

- *I don't know how to position sexuality with my content, or story, or characters, so I leave it out.*

- *Should I have the people talk to each other during sex?*

- *I'm scared of what others will think about me if I write sex. They'll think I do the things I write.*

If you have uttered statements or questions like these, you are not alone. Even best-selling authors feel that way. I designed this book to help you address these types of concerns, bond readers with your characters, and gain confidence as you work.

Let me tell you the story of how this book came to be and what you'll gain from reading it.

The Book Idea Crystallizes

In the fall of 2018, I presented my first sexuality writing workshops to writers at the Florida Writers Association Annual Conference. The questions and feedback I received solidified what my then forty-two years of sexuality work had taught me.

Writers' concerns about writing sexuality reflected the same sexuality concerns of everyday people.

On the drive home, I considered writers' statements from the conference, which were filled with the same feelings I had heard from other writers, and I sat with a key idea.

People fear what they don't know.

And sexuality may be one of the scariest things of all because, not only is it often unknown, but it is also laced with the shame and guilt of our upbringing, our religion, and our culture. No one taught us how to keep negative biases or misinformation out of our work, much less how to use sexuality content and knowledge to craft our characters with intention.

When I arrived home from the conference, my family announced something incredible. They told me, of all things, that John Grisham needed my help.

What? How was that even *possible*?

My family members had watched Grisham's (2018) interview about his book, *The Reckoning*, on *CBS This Morning*. Toward the end of the discussion, the interviewer mentioned that he seemed to rely on his wife's advice about sex scenes. There, on national television, he admitted he couldn't write sex scenes, and he said his wife had laughed at one he wrote years before. He lamented it was too hard and better suited for women to write. He asked, "You get two people who—it's time for them to go to bed, and then what are you supposed—am I supposed to describe body parts or something?" (Check out the interview from 3:48–4:33: https://www.youtube.com/watch?v=FkUyakxQFcU.)

Yay, for my family supporting me and knowing what it is I do. They expected I would have some specific things to say about his statements. Of course I did. I replayed his words and stacked them against all the other conversations I had ever had about sexuality writing since I began my writing journey. Not only do people fear what they don't know, but they avoid it, too. These two ideas shifted around in my head, giving me the signal that I had something new to offer.

What Do I Know That Other Writers Don't?

People ask me about sexuality in writing all the time, especially when they find out about my extensive sexuality background. My closest writer friends seek my opinion during regular discussions on the topic of sexuality. But it wasn't until the Florida Writers Association conference coordinator asked me to present that the gears started turning. Before that, I had even dismissed a writer colleague who insisted I write this book. I needed a lot of messages to push me down this path.

When the messages merged the day I returned home from the conference, I finally understood. I could create a guide to help people understand sexuality in writing so they wouldn't have to fear (and avoid) it. What tipped the balance? John Grisham's video? Or maybe it was the day I found myself sitting in a Panera with *New York Times* best-selling author and fellow Florida State University alum, Alessandra Torre; when I shared my idea to write about scenes with sex, she enthusiastically supported it. It may have been the fact that nearly a dozen editors had selected my short stories for publication.

Perhaps it was when Rosy Wellness, a sexual health business with a grounded focus on sexuality research, asked me to write and teach about erotica for them. They have since hired me as their erotica editor.

In the end, maybe it was the sheer accumulation of all those things. And with every good story, the protagonist needs obstacles. Once the reality existed that I would write this book, a fresh voice of inadequacy boomed in my head.

Who do you think you are? Why do you think you can do this?

Imposter syndrome had reared its head. Doubt has a way of creeping in.

My own voice surprised me when I uttered these words aloud: "Me? Write about sexuality or scenes with sex?" I laughed. "I'm not qualified."

When I shared this self-talk with my closest author friends, they looked at me like I had grown two heads. The interrogation started.

"Dr. J., how do you spend your days?"

"I write erotica."

"And in writing erotica, what is your primary focus?"

"I write about sexuality and scenes with sex."

I couldn't see the forest for the trees, but I could tell you a lot about the tree bark.

Hmm. Perhaps I knew something about this topic. After all, with four and a half decades of sexuality know-how under my belt from my work as a human-sexuality professor, a licensed sex therapist, and a sexuality consultant, I might have a few things to say on the subject. I might even know more than John Grisham.

And perhaps it was time to get on with it, like all writers must.

Clarifying My Task—and Owning It

To start, I reflected on and honored my path to becoming a fiction writer. I had never written fiction before 2016, and I wasn't sure how my professional experience would translate. So, like many novice writers, I took classes.

My first one was a basic class on what I needed to know about writing scenes with sex for erotica and erotic fiction. Then I attended editing classes, novel-writing classes, and lots of webinars about the craft of writing, all the while staying focused on sexuality.

As I wrote, elements appeared on the page that I understood. The experience was not unlike how I had processed sexuality information before. For me, writing characters was much like therapy. They were my clients, and I applied my sex therapy training to them.

Before the conference and John Grisham video, an author friend asked me to assess her manuscript for consistency between its psychological aspects and descriptions of sexuality. When I had finished reading and looked at my notes, they surprised me. I had read her manuscript as if the protagonist was my client. I had outlined the content of his life like I would write therapy notes.

Afterward, I shared my notes with my friend. Where characters were inconsistent, I offered additional ideas for their backgrounds so the behaviors she had written would feel organic and genuine. She was thrilled with the level of detail, and my notes helped her bring the characters forward in a new way.

Even this experience didn't push me to write the book. And guess what? In real life and fiction alike, the catalyst must fit to get an individual to move. We all get to our get-on-with-it moments from different paths. For me, it took the combination of teaching other writers and hearing Grisham's interview to realize the time had come to share my paradigm with you.

What You Are Getting

Because of my integrated sexuality training, I approach sexuality with more information than most. But you can educate yourself—it's never too late to learn.

Mostly, writers and non-writers alike receive no formal comprehensive sexuality education in the United States. This reality is a common thread, and it shows up in the ideas you have when it comes to writing about sexuality. You don't know what you don't know. But you can know, and I can break down the information for you.

Whether you are crafting a scene of solo sex, partner sex, or group sex, and whatever gender and sexual orientation the people in that scene represent, my sexuality background provides fresh ways to conceptualize the story, the characters, the setting of sex, and the portrayal of sex. This book is a road map to help you navigate the layers of your characters' sexuality in order to give those characters new depth and realism.

Returning to our weaving analogy: You have threads, and you must anchor them to your project from the start. I'll show you how to see sexuality as one of those threads and appreciate its value in developing characters for meaningful story and scene.

You may have come here for a "sex scene" talk, but you will leave with *so much more*.

As with all work, writing itself is a journey. My journey led me here. Let me now be your guide and help you integrate the worlds of sexuality and story craft. I offer you education, a new paradigm, and sexuality templates so you can pick up the thread of sex with confidence as you weave the tapestry of your story.

FRAME YOUR SEXUALITY WRITING—A PARADIGM SHIFT

Session 1   Sex-Positive Sexuality

Choosing to Write Sexuality with Intent

How you frame a topic—how you create or plan it—depends on the perspective you use.

Where sexuality is concerned, most people, regardless of whether they are writers or not, never receive the tools to frame sexuality with *intent*, for themselves or others. Without such training, you may present what I call a "cloudy lens." This occurs because most people have never experienced comprehensive sexuality education or training in sexuality. Without this instruction, you may never realize what you need in order to frame your work in a world larger than or different from yours. With schooling, you can put yourself in the driver's seat and develop full characters for us to enjoy.

In the United States, people without comprehensive sexuality education assimilate their beliefs about sexuality from the surrounding world. You may have learned about it from your friends, parents, religious affiliations, TV, the internet, or experiences with other people. Typically, in American culture, that means you received a judgmental, fear-based, and shame-based sexuality education. It could have been covert or overt. Without knowing, you may be influenced by this in your writing.

You know what I mean.

Shhh. Don't talk about that.

You can't say that word.

Sex is only for procreation.

Never mind basic facts about the body, like the clitoris only having one function: pleasure. Or the fact that the clitoris is actually a clitoral body with three distinct parts housed in different areas of the pelvis: internal, hugging the vagina, and external within the vulva. Knowing or not knowing details information like this informs your writing.

The clitoral body is but one factual example of things people often don't know about sexuality. This list goes on, and it is compiled based on where you were brought up, who you knew, and what your experiences were. I hope to bring awareness to all areas of sexuality. This discussion can mark the place of your personal knowledge and understanding. You can recognize that you know the facts or you don't.

I hear many authors address the "sex scene," but that phrase shows only one aspect of the total picture. I want to show you how to write with a full view of sex from the beginning of your story. When writers do this, they draw on information to help them create the best possible fiction story, beginning to end, with sexuality playing an equal role to all the other elements of their characters, whether it's in the foreground or background.

And in terms of your writing style, it doesn't matter whether you are a "pantser" (one who writes without an outline) or "plotter" (one who creates and writes from an outline). This is a template you can use as you're writing or after you've written your first draft. Either way, it's a tool to help you evaluate the emphasis you have on sex in your story. You'll have control over where sexuality goes and how it unfolds, much like composing visual art. What is in the foreground and the background? Which way enhances your story at a particular juncture?

You've heard as a writer, "Write what you know." In the sexuality arena, writing what you know about sexuality may not get you what you want. But if you write with intent, you'll go far in making meaning for the character and the story.

Expanding Your Sexuality Awareness

Let me share a personal life story about framing sexuality. I hope it will highlight for you the connection between personal experiences and larger societal structures.

Many years ago, my partner split his kidney in a motorcycle accident and it involved a trip to the hospital. Surgery repaired the problem, and all is well and good there.

Before I get to the sexuality part of the story, I need you to know that a good portion of my private practice work involved consulting with medical providers, doctors, nurses, physician assistants, and family nurse practitioners to assess their knowledge and then provide sex-positive educational training.

Now back to the motorcycle story.

The setting was the patient room in the hospital, complete with lingering antiseptic odors and wiggly green Jell-O. The sexuality event occurred at the time of my partner's discharge. The surgeon arrived to discharge him and discuss detailed post-op instructions. I collected all the paperwork for home. They gave my love lots of physical dos and don'ts. And guess what? Nowhere in this paperwork did they address sex.

Being the model partner and sexuality expert extraordinaire, I asked the doctor this follow-up question: "When will my partner be able to take part in sexual behaviors, either solo or coupled?"

Even today, thinking of my question throws me back into that room. A pins-and-needles sensation surfaces on my skin, and heat runs through my body.

As my question hung in the air, the surgeon laughed and then beamed at both of us. "Well, if your sex life is anything like mine, it doesn't matter."

I still shiver at this sentence. The surgeon's answer should not have stunned me, but it did.

It did so because it was personal. It was about my partner, his life, and our life. Instead of factual information, we received personal information from the doctor.

My world moved in slow motion.

I had trained myself to see teachable moments in sexuality events as they occurred. I imagined how the writers of the children's classic *The Berenstain Bears* would help me. They'd caption this scene in my hospital story, lined up for their classic cautionary-tale lesson style, with their famous line in a cartoon bubble over my head: *This is what you must not do, so let that be a lesson to you.*

As a sexuality teacher and therapist suspended in this cartoon bubble, I cringed like I had heard fingernails on a blackboard.

I have a visceral response when I see a sexual injustice inflicted on another. At least I understood what was happening. And I have said, time after time, better for it to happen to me than someone who doesn't know how to evaluate the information they are getting.

My reply: "Thanks for nothing. I'll figure it out myself."

I continue to recycle this event as a teachable moment and use it for good. Like now. It drives home the point that talking about what you don't know is not helpful. In fact, it can be harmful.

What did the doctor's answer mean? With his attitude, content, and perspective? He sent this message: *Sexuality must not matter much.*

Clearly, the doctor had received no sexuality bedside-manner training. This is an example of an unintended message being wired into us through the emotionality of a situation. Some emotional experience became entwined in his body with this content—sex doesn't matter much.

The physician considered his response innocuous, using humor to cover up his discomfort, ignorance, and lack of training. I believe the response was unconscious. And this was someone who you and the general population probably would have believed had been educated about sexuality.

In the early years of my career, when I worked with physicians, they received about ten hours of sexuality training in medical school and residency. Today, that has dwindled to about one hour and typically addresses male sexuality.

These are people at the highest level of education, not receiving sexuality information. What about everyone else?

As a writer, you most likely have not received education about writing sex in terms of meaningful placement and content.

I use this story to illustrate how easy it is to answer questions negatively, incorrectly, or personally, if that's all you know or have experienced. As a writer, you may not know how to set up sexual events that are realistic or factual. Or perhaps you write a certain way because that's how it's always been done.

But it is also easy to answer questions and write positively if you're trained and you learn how.

By embracing a broader informed perspective, you can learn how to deliver a sexuality message in a voice that will resonate with readers in a respectful, connected, and understanding manner.

In Session 2, when I introduce the Person of the Writer, I will discuss how you can embody that in your work and your own life. In this way, you can see that I've continued "figuring it out myself."

I'm now in a position where I can take the personal lessons and effect change on the other areas that impact my life. In this chapter, I'll apply them to the structure of writing.

Throughout this guide, I'll provide places for you to stop and ask yourself questions. You can begin your personal assessment of your sexuality with some basic self-reflection. Let's practice that here.

Author Self-Reflection Questions

Your Context

Sometimes you go to other people for information. How do other people help you make the connections you need for sexuality in your story?

MY SEXUAL AWARENESS AND MINDSET

What are my attitudes about sex?

What topics might I be judgmental or dismissive about? Why?

Am I able to address, understand, and hold both sides of the sexuality coin?

Are my words inclusive of all people and behaviors?

How would I assess my attitudes toward sex in my writing?

I'd like you to stop and consider an element of communication. Generally, when a person speaks, the content delivered is based on their experiences, attitudes, and beliefs. Their communication is specific to those things. Therefore, when you ask other people questions about writing, you may not receive answers that relate to your specific writing process, characters, or event material.

Recently I saw a memoir author ask other authors what words she should use when her sixteen-year-old self is talking about sex in her story. One author suggested she ask other people what to use. Another author suggested going to YA books and copying what they provide. Notice that these answers were separate from the context of what the *author* was writing about—herself.

Here was my response: "What words would your sixteen-year-old-self know and/or use? I create words in *context* of the character's age, time frame in life, sex history, etc."

I hear authors ask other authors questions about how to write sexuality. The answers they give are statements about themselves. Many times, they provide brilliant answers, but if you only get answers that are personal or based on what everyone else has done, how do you move past the status quo of writing sex? Using a new paradigm to think about sexuality will help. Remember, your story is about the characters and their experiences.

Author Self-Reflection on What Others Say

Do you assess how others came up with their answer?

What assumptions are they drawing on?

Typical answers include:

That's how I've done it.

That's how it's always done.

I value reassessment and evaluation. You can always improve on your writing, in any genre, and in turn improve the portrayal of sexuality in your story.

Begin the New Thinking Process

Let's start simply. Every topic has at least two sides, even sexuality. It is helpful to your writing to see both sides of the sexuality coin. If you have lived one side (fear- and shame-based sexuality) what does the other side (a sex-positive perspective) look like? When you can understand and access both viewpoints, you can consciously choose how to portray sexuality in your writing and know the reasons behind your choices. This way you are not bound by the systems you grew up in; you can see the way you were taught, and you can see another perspective. In our context, this is an example of a macro lens, which will be part of your learning in Session 3.

So, do you think you can hold the perspectives of both sides of the coin simultaneously? This is a learned skill, but once learned, it will serve you well in your writing. You'll understand the tension created from different and even polar positions. Let me share a story about holding the two perspectives and presenting to an audience.

Hold Multiple Perspectives

In the late-90s, The Florida State University Theatre Department at The Lab Theatre performed Paula Vogel's work, *How I Learned to Drive*. The play's theme was about the experience of sexual abuse, and Vogel used the metaphor of driving to discuss control and manipulation. The director of the play had concerns about how the actors and the patrons would experience the sexual content, and they contacted me. They asked me to talk with the actors about how to process the content they were acting out, because these college students were stepping into the skin of both the abused and the abuser.

It takes a lot of courage and self-development (called differentiation, which you'll learn about in Session 8) to hold both perspectives of abuse. It takes individual capacity to understand that the abuser was once abused. This play provides an overview of a sexual abuse event spanning four generations, showing how the abused individuals perpetuated the cycle of abuse in the play, an abused child becomes an abusing uncle, who abuses his niece, who abuses a younger man. I held all those perspectives in my head as I explained the process to the actors.

While the content of abuse is not sex-positive, the treatment, and even discussion of it can be. I was there to help the actors process their feelings. I was there to assist the patrons in processing theirs as well when the show concluded. It was an opportunity to shine a light on another way to address issues that arise in the context of sex, in real time, and respond with kindness and compassion. So, in the writing context, you can consider how to bring content forward in the same way.

I use this as an example because, in your life, events have impacted you. And, as was the case for the doctor in the hospital room, those events wire the emotionality of the situation into you. You may or may not have the skills to be resilient in your response, but when you learn about a new way, you can develop them.

To learn more about *How I Learned to Drive*, visit the play's Wikipedia page: https://en.wikipedia.org/wiki/How_I_Learned_to_Drive.

Defining a Sex-Positive Attitude

What is the definition of **sex-positive**? What does being sex-positive look like? What are the components?

Being trained as a sexuality educator and sex therapist allowed me many years to assimilate my ideas of what sex positivity is and how to embody it, in behavior and in words. Here's my code:

My sex-positive frame is an overarching philosophy.

It recognizes sexuality as a natural and healthy aspect of one's life.

It supports consensual sexual behaviors that are pleasurable to the parties involved.

It respects how individuals define themselves and their relationships.

It employs empathy in understanding individuals' struggles based on different-ness.

A sex-positive stance is active. It presents a way for people to see sexuality as a constructive force in their lives, and it celebrates sexual diversity. This is the opposite of a **sex-negative** stance, which focuses on the nature of sexuality being problematic, dangerous, or disruptive, and which may be so ingrained in your thinking that you don't see it there.

In a blog post, sex researcher Justin Lehmiller (2019) outlines his eight-part definition of the term sex-positive from his book, *The Psychology of Human Sexuality* (2018). The first part is: "Adopting comprehensive and inclusive definitions of gender and sexual orientation."

I highlight this point because, in sexuality work, it is important to be nonjudgmental and open in discussing sexuality. It may not even be in your checklist to consider how you've been emotionally wired due to an event or experience related to sexual diversity. When you realize there is a continuum for attitudes, behaviors, and types of relationships, and that people may choose to engage or not engage, experience something or not experience something, then you begin working the idea into yourself and your writing.

Why talk about this?

It's simple. When you write, you teach.

I saw evidence of this all the time in classrooms, the therapy office, or in doctors' exam rooms. You assimilate information from what is in front of you. Most people don't seek an understanding of sexuality for themselves unless they feel they are different, there is a pressing concern, or someone is not happy with them. Then the nagging need to define oneself becomes the impetus for seeking information and help in sexuality.

I heard people share how they learned about sex from reading romance novels and getting to "the good parts."

I heard people talk about their visual learning through adult erotic films.

I heard people talk about sex from their experience as if that experience belonged to everyone.

You bring forth your sexual work either with intent or without.

Are you writing on purpose or by accident?

In your writing, are you perpetuating only the side of the coin that casts sex negatively, or are you opening the sexuality world for examination?

If you haven't been taught about sexuality in a sex-positive way, then you haven't learned how to bring it forward with intention. So, what have you brought forward instead? You have brought forward whatever you have learned from your life.

Accurate or inaccurate pieces of information live in you. Do you know if you are perpetuating myths and misinformation when you write? Do you perhaps omit details of sexuality because they are too difficult to address?

Instead, you can identify and clear your personal expectations, assumptions, and biases in order to write openly and honestly about sexuality or create accurate sexual experiences for your characters.

Writing from Macro and Micro Lens Positions

When you are working with a **macro lens**, you pull back and look at the entire story—the overall story plot. You are probably familiar with this as a developmental component of writing. With your macro lens, you can ask yourself: Did you attach sexuality at the beginning of your writing and then weave it throughout? Or did you only put sexuality in the obligatory and expected places, pulling it off the shelf to use once or twice?

Were your hero and supporting characters presented as fully formed, holistic characters, with sexuality included?

Can you recognize them based on their sexuality?

When you employ your **micro lens**, you are working at the scene level. In each scene, you can ask yourself: Are you choosing details to accentuate sexuality? And do you understand the reasons you put them there?

When I supervised therapy students and students studying child development, it was necessary to ask those two questions. How did they choose a specific action or specific words, and why? I looked for their application of the process and their understanding of the process. These questions are exactly the same for a writer.

If you understand how something works theoretically, then you control it instead of it controlling you. As a writer, you are always learning new information about how to write better stories. Now you can address the often-ignored element of sexuality.

Whether you are writing a scene with sex, or writing sex throughout the entire story, you can control it. It is more than "Sex sells." It is more than "It's supposed to be in this spot."

Use this "mind skill" touted by my friend, George Silverman (2023): Be aware of and adjust your mental processes while you are still "in them." This is a metacognition ability where you are aware of and understand your thoughts and patterns as you write. With the information I am presenting, you can add sexuality to your metacognitive assessments.

For sexuality, that could mean switching from your biases to a mode of openness. Your ability to assess your sexuality work from both macro and micro vantage points will allow you to see it for what it is.

Session 2   The Person or Self of the Writer

Introduction

What do you, as a writer, bring of yourself to writing about sexuality as a whole? To answer this, use your macro lens and look at all of your life until now.

What do you bring to writing a specific scene with sex? To answer this, use a micro lens and look at all of your specific sexual experiences until now.

I can tell you, and you probably already believe, that when you write anything about sex, some folks are going to think you have experienced it.

A New Perspective

If I write about murder, does that mean I've committed one? Even if you are a fiction writer crafting a story based on your creativity and imagination, others, because of how their Selves are constructed, will believe your character is you. I make this comment so you can prepare yourself. Yet, when you have done the deep dive into the work of writing sex, you'll find you will have strengthened the part of yourself that is separate and clear from what other people have to say.

While I say this as a cautionary tale, take heart. It speaks volumes about the need to understand the sexual Self and how it affects your writing. And think of it this way: You can always leave other folks guessing. As the writer, just as a pilot, you are in charge of the transportation on this journey.

My Origin Story of the Person or Self of the Writer

Here's a story of where the power of this concept, my Writer Self, crystallized in my life. It occurred during my doctoral program. I learned about the **Person or Self of the Writer** long before I intellectually understood what it was or even thought I would one day write fiction or nonfiction with sexuality elements.

The professor who taught my graduate human-sexuality course assigned a theoretical application paper. Specifically, I had to discuss abortion through six different theoretical constructs. The goal of this assignment was to apply the theories without a hint of the personal ideology of my Writer Self.

I received the ever coveted full one hundred points on the paper. This teacher never gave that score. I was ecstatic.

As she handed my paper to me, she asked me to stay after class. I didn't know what to expect. Butterflies wreaked havoc in my stomach. This professor was an icon in the field, and I didn't want to ruffle any feathers or disappoint. I couldn't imagine what she wanted to talk about. Everyone left the room, and I stayed seated, my winged soiree surging in my belly. She walked over and sat down beside me.

"I had to read your paper several times to glean there was no hint of your personal position. It was amazing—nothing was there. You must be a great therapist; clients would never feel judged by you."

Her statement stunned me, and I thanked her profusely. We chatted a little more, and I stood to leave for my next class.

When I got to the door, she called after me, "So, what is your position on abortion?"

I turned and smiled. "That information wasn't part of the assignment."

Later, I discovered from subsequent students that the professor used my writing as an example for teaching this topic. I worked hard on that paper in order to meet the assignment requirements and keep my personal thoughts out. This assignment was the moment when separating my sexual Self from my writing anchored itself to my personal sex history timeline.

How Did I Write the Paper and Meet the Expectation?

I didn't know it, but to write the theoretical paper, I used what I now call the **Three-Self Concept**: Knowledge of Self, Access to Self, and Management of Self (Aponte 2016). This way of thinking had been part of the five-year training in my first job.

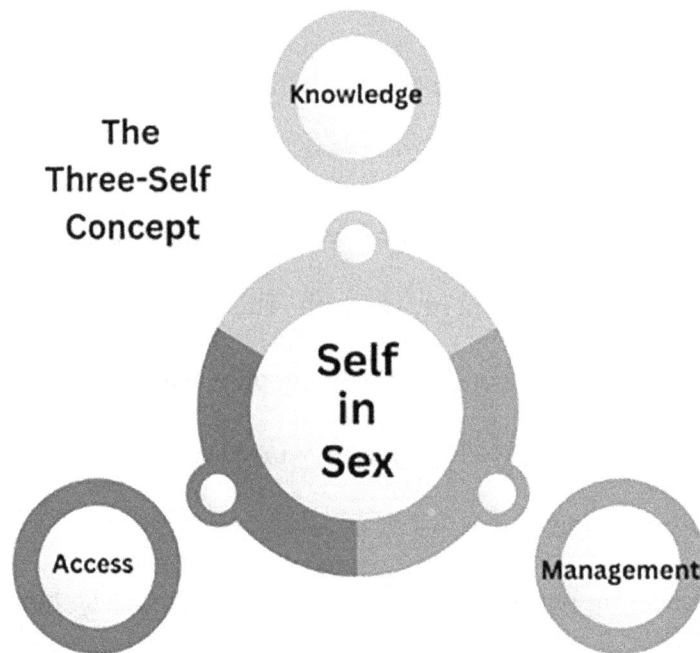

These three areas have helped me focus on writing sex, and I hope you'll find they help you, too.

The Three-Self Concept

Knowledge of Self in Sex

Knowledge of Self in sex is a working understanding of what you believe, think, and construct about sexuality. This may be based on your experiences, and the sources of this knowledge may be marked on your personal sex history timeline. Knowledge may have arrived from all the elements that make up the holistic sexual person. The four elements of the holistic sexual person are called the physical, emotional, mental, and spiritual components, or PEMS for short. Information, experiences, facts, and scripts all live in these areas. These are your content files of sexuality, and if you have not labeled them, now is the perfect time.

Access to Self in Sex

Access to Self in sex is the idea that, in response to different topics, you can locate your experiences, thoughts, feelings, wants, and desires. You can tap into PEMS content, which makes the information accessible for your use. Since emotion is the glue that connects readers to your story, and to sex in your story, it is important that you have access to a range of emotions within *your* Self. This allows you to tap into and amplify the emotions your characters experience. This process differs from your characters experiencing only what you have experienced, which is what other folks may think.

Management of Self in Sex

Management of Self in sex is about establishing clarity in where your personal boundaries stop and start. Think of it as a circle around you, at arm's length: Everything inside the circle is you and your Self. Everything outside the circle is not you.

Create the Trifecta

For writing, you can use the Three-Self Concept for each component of PEMS, but I posit you will know which one of these components can take the lead in your writing. You probably have a good idea of which areas have more conscious material in them. Consider this as part of your internal process when you create characters. The story you are crafting is about what happens to the characters. Unless you are writing memoir, you will only use portions of your personal sex history content in your writing. It is identifying the separation of your growth from your characters' growth that matters.

Each area allows you to be intentional in what you bring forward. The more overt knowledge you have of your sexual Self, the more you can access your sexual Self and manage *your* Self. You can create a trifecta of personal reserves to stockpile in your writer's toolbox. The clarity you have in each area, coupled with intentionality around their use, strengthens your writing outcome. When you remain flexible with your feelings and attitudes, you have a special fuel with which to write created just for you.

What do these concepts—Knowledge of Self, Access to Self, and Management of Self— look like in writing?

A Case Study: "Infused Leather"

Link: *https://qr1.be/X9TE*

Let me introduce you to my short erotic story, "Infused Leather," which was published in *Best Women's Erotica of the Year Volume 3* in 2017.

It was my first published piece. I was proud and elated when the *Best Women's Erotica of the Year* series got a starred review in both *Publishers Weekly* and the *Library Journal*. My heart sang when *Publishers Weekly* mentioned my story by name in their review and the *Library Journal* mentioned it by theme. With these accolades, I submitted the story for a writing competition.

If you are concerned about how other people will take your writing, this macro story is about my process. I offer it as an example and an application of the sexuality concepts discussed so far. For context, I'm an author who has utilized all the concepts I address in this book.

This story is about how a writing competition judge approached my submission. Like the doctor in the hospital room, it was clear the judge had no experience with sexuality. I had wondered about that prior to submitting, but so much more than I could have known came through in the feedback. Let me also add that my story could go forward in the competition only if it contained specific narrative components of writing. Since the story had been accepted, it had already been established that it met the writing competition criteria.

Present Conflict

Unlike many stories I've written, "Infused Leather" came fully formed. It is a story of personal redemption through sexual choices. So, I was thrown when the judge commented that there was no present conflict in the story.

As a sex therapist, the model of therapy I practiced was about healing past wounds in present time. It was about stepping into yourself and making specific choices in real time that would overcome the wounds of the past. My characters had sexual abuse histories I didn't need to address explicitly. They were there, residing in the characters, influencing how they were in the world. Those histories were part of who they were—words, thoughts, deeds, and actions.

And just like in therapy, I didn't need to have the clients go back over their history. I helped them move through their pain, guiding them to triumph in their everyday life, identify what they wanted, and go after those desires. The fictional couple in "Infused Leather," through their sexual choices together, create a way to go right through the past problems and come out the other side as changed people.

BDSM vs. Leather Fetish

This competition feedback reminded me of when I started my doctoral program. No one could supervise me because I had more sex therapy experience than they did. The judge had also incorrectly categorized my story as BDSM (Bondage and Discipline, Dominance and submission, and Sadism and Masochism), when it was, instead, a leather fetish story. The characters took abusive leather events of the past and turned them into something positive.

The Average Person

The judge further commented that no average person would have even read two pages of the story, much less ever related to the story. However, taking control of your sexuality and doing what you want is a huge component of understanding yourself. It places a value on sexuality as a quality-of-life component.

Who can't understand that? Possibly someone who is not actively and intentionally using the Three-Self Concept. The feedback indicated a mind closed to sexuality.

Bias vs. Empathy

Life goes full circle. I used to work for Adam and Eve; now I work with a writer and director for Adam and Eve. My sexuality work used to not be understood; now my writing is not understood. The existing levels of shame and intolerance of differences keep us from understanding a wide range of human sexual experiences.

The judge's feedback brought to mind all the work I have done on empathy.

What is it to struggle? What is it to be in someone else's shoes? Science shows us these types of empathetic connections light up in your brain.

Was the judge so blinded by cultural, personal, and negative biases that they wouldn't allow themself to experience my story and the scenes with sex? They put the "no" on from the beginning, and that was all they wrote.

Typical vs. Atypical

Two different editors worked with me on this story before the final editor selected it for publication. My confidence was high when it came to the writing components. But the sexuality aspects were atypical of a leather fetish story. I was writing a story that could have occurred in the real lives of two people creating their own reality and learning and growing together.

This judge called my work typical and trite. Really?

Story Arc

I constructed the story based on character development through sexuality—a true sexual journey—the essence of which is simple: How do you move and grow and get what you want out of sex? I portray the change. Yes, the characters' original conflicts live in the past, but a past conflict lives every day with someone until they choose to resolve it. Showing two people moving forward together through making a choice to face their conflicts shows that redemption is possible on an individual's own terms. It also comes from a place of strength, not fear. The characters wanted more for each other.

I was told by the judge there was no story arc. My characters, Angie and Harold, sexual abuse survivors, change the meaning of their past sexual history in the present. The action of changing the past in the present is a story arc, to me. Getting a perpetrator's voice out of your head through your own actions is a story arc. The characters aren't the same at the start of the story as they are at the end.

You can tell, I'm sure, that the impact of this writing competition event created additional personal fuel to use as a teaching lesson. This is what talented writers do: find and use the fuel for good. Now that you have seen how I applied my framework to the judge's remarks, I hope it allows you to see another piece of the sex writing puzzle that set the stage for the book.

Application of the Three-Self Concept to This Story

Knowledge of Self

Let's consider the factual element: BDSM vs. fetish kink. The judge held incorrect information about sexuality. Their discussion of the concepts was incorrect.

Access to Self and Management of Self

The judge made points about how other people would respond: first, that no average person would read past two pages, and second, that people wouldn't relate to the story.

To start, the judge breached a boundary when the used themself as the measuring stick, of reader response.

And then, the judge put a judgment from their Self on the story. If, with an open mind, they had read the story to see that the two people consensually changed the meaning of sex for themselves, they might have sat with the emotion of the transforming nature and humanity of those actions. This example illustrates the idea that access to and understanding of what you think, feel, and believe are necessary when analyzing other work.

Could the judge have taken the competition template and applied the rubric without offering these statements in their feedback of my story. Yes. Two other judges did that in their responses to me. Part of our responsibility is an open-mindedness to sexuality, and considering whether we shame or berate others because of it.

Another part is knowing and owning where we stand on topics. Could the judge have said "pass" and let someone else read? Yes.

Takeaways

In some ways, working on your Self is about focus, but in other ways it is about becoming clear on how you think about sexuality. Perhaps you have learned or will learn to embrace the idea that sexuality has so much to offer. It could become the perspective you hold. Perhaps you have learned or will learn not to dismiss the overarching idea of sexuality or think it shouldn't be there. If you understand where *you* are with the topic, it will be easier to see where the characters are with the topic. This may also be the start of understanding clear boundaries for consent in your stories.

I expect you have lots of feelings and questions for yourself. That is good. If you hold on to *your* Self when sexuality makes you uncomfortable, you, like the characters, can come out on the other side changed. Your writing will be richer if you understand the why of all the forward movement of your characters. I want you to learn to apply this to the character's sexual Self and their actions.

You may think this is a hard task, but each of us starts somewhere. For me, it's what I know, but that's been cultivated. It's where I've worked for years. It's where I'm comfortable. I know the vast majority of the world is not in that place. I've worked very hard to create the permission-giving and nonjudgmental stance on sexuality that everyone deserves. And I hope I can give you the needed information to create that for yourself.

You can't escape your history unless you openly work with yourself. Your biases may come through in your writing. So how do you check them?

The Case for Creating your Own Comprehensive Sexuality Education

It's for your characters, right? Because most of us have had no comprehensive sexuality education, it's important to understand that as writers, as I mentioned before, we teach when we write. How do I know this? *As a therapist*, when I asked clients how they learned about sex, reading novels was a frequent answer. *As a human-sexuality teacher*, when I asked students how they learned about sex, reading novels was a frequent answer. Your writing teaches. You can choose to leave the reader better than when they started. They may not know you planted good sex seeds, but you will! So, I invite you to write with *intention.*

If your character was going to skydive and you knew nothing about it, you would go study and get the needed information. Lots of times, characters put us on the road to learning. But often, there is no template for a writer to position their sexuality information.

For the Person of the Writer, let's start with three areas:

Is my writing fictionally realistic? Factually accurate?

Can my sexual multilingual skills shine?

Can I minimize author intrusion?

Reflection 1: The Facts

Is your sex writing fictionally realistic? Factually correct?

Just stick to the facts. Nothing gets me going more than inaccurate sex information in a book. It pulls me out of the experience I'm having.

Fact-Checking Examples

In the following examples, the term **cisgender** refers to people who identify with the sex assigned to them at birth (Kinkly 2019).

- Imagine a romance involving a cisgender woman: Closed-door sex leads to the woman's first pregnancy. The woman's water breaks. Contractions are immediately thirty seconds apart. The baby is delivered in fifteen minutes. Accurate or inaccurate?

- Does your method of orgasming perpetuate the myth that people with vulvas have orgasms through **penis-in-vagina (PinV) intercourse** alone? Please stop. Research shows most people with vulvas need additional clitoral stimulation.

- Do you understand the cycle of sexual response? After a person with a penis ejaculates and orgasms, how much of a break do they need before getting another erection? They need recovery time for the body to re-pump blood to the pelvis. The amount of time varies depending on age and health.

Don't know something? Research it. My web history is interesting. Yours?

When you begin sex research, locate resources that are factually accurate and sex-positive. Are your resources reputable? Use people that know more scientific information than you. (This gets interesting if you are creating worlds without human sex norms. You must then create the full sexual world and decide how it works.)

Reflection 2: Multilingual Skills

Can your sexual multilingual skills shine?

I can't say that word.

Why can't you say it? Do you have language biases? Consider that you are multilingual in sex with lots of language categories. Accurate. Medical. Slang. Baby talk. Always know why you use a specific word. It should fit with the character's language and beliefs, not the author's comfort.

A Story About Language Bias

I presented a sexuality workshop for parents at a preschool. One area of discussion was using accurate language. In the first nine months of a child's life, adults can practice using accurate language along with just the right tone before the child understands the language. At nine months, receptive language develops, and the child understands some words. It is after nine months that expressive language occurs and they begin to use the words for themselves.

I went through several scenarios for the parents. One example I discussed was bowel movements in toddlerhood.

It's important to understand that I use many educational templates to help folks understand where sexuality fits in the world. For children (and their parents), I look at their specific system developments, including speech. One parent insisted their child couldn't possibly say "bowel movement" or "urinate." I knew the child being referred to, and I knew they loved dinosaurs. I asked the parent to name all the dinosaurs the child could name. They obliged and recited a list proudly.

What do you think I did with that information?

I went to PEMS, and I addressed the mental and physical capability templates for a child of that age. This child understood the different dinosaurs' labels. They could formulate the word pattern through speech. I extrapolated the child's ability to use sexuality vocabulary from the child's ability to name dinosaurs.

How many syllables was that child able to say? Tri-cer-a-tops. I counted syllables. Ur-i-nate. Bow-el move-ment.

So, the belief that children can't use accurate language is not about the child's PEMS capabilities. It's about the parents' discomfort, shame, or lack of education surrounding sexuality words.

I use this specific example to show you that emotion, sexual scripts, beliefs, and your upbringing sit with you in your decisions. Any words can be used within the context of the character, setting, education, etc. You, as the author, need to know why you are using them. Are they part of the world of the character? Your work is about teasing your words apart so you, the author, can be confident in why you choose what you choose in your stories that involve sex. And for sex specifically, are you promoting sex-positive words and tone?

Reflection 3: Author Intrusion

Can you minimize author intrusion? Can you have clear boundaries between you and your characters?

I often hear my editor's voice about author intrusion: "Is that the author talking?"

Think like an actor. Ask, "Did I slip out of character?" Your story is the place where you practice getting out of your own way. Look for *assumptions* and *biases* in your thinking about sexuality. *Challenge* yourself.

You write stuff you haven't done before. Don't worry about that—research can give you the how-tos. Even if you haven't done something, you have experienced the *feeling* that is wired into the action you are creating. That's the part of *You* that you *do* use to write sex in a scene. The balance comes from using the three areas of Self.

A Paradigm Shift

If you identify as cisgender and heterosexual, consider the following questions: When did you know you were heterosexual? When did you know you were cisgender?

- Have you entertained these questions?
- Has anyone ever asked you these questions?
- Did you experience cognitive dissonance from the questions?
- Do the questions shift something in your thinking?

If you identify as LGBTQ+, this is part of your life. It's an interesting question, as so many use the converse type of question routinely: When did you know you were gay? Bisexual?

When a queer person comes out, they talk about knowing when, why. It's because we, as a culture, have made it a negative script. The cisgender/heterosexual (cishet) script is sanctioned as normal. But if cishet people apply the same questions—when did you know you were cisgender, when did you know you were heterosexual—then they can activate more areas of their Self to make their characters (and their life) fuller.

Brian McNaught, a longtime colleague, a prominent sexuality diversity trainer, and the author of *On Being Gay and Gray*, talks about why people need to understand the experience of being gay. He is the champion of empathy and teaching you how to put yourself in someone else's shoes, and he could be a great resource for you.

What is it like to grow up in the world being gay, or intersex, or nonbinary, or bisexual or trans or genderqueer? Where is the empathy to understand those potential struggles, individuals face when they claim who they are for themselves and with a witness?

Regarding gender in particular, here is a resource to help you assess your gender bias: https://thepsychologygroup.com/how-hidden-gender-biases-harm-the-lgbtq-community/.

Conclusion

The Person or Self of the Writer is uniquely you. When you take the time to understand *your* Self—especially your sexual Self—in the context of what your imagination cooks up for a story, you will have so much more to work with.

Enjoy the self-exploration journey as you learn and grow. I love it when one aspect of growth impacts another. And when any question related to identity is asked, check your heteronormative stance at the door.

Session 3 The Components of Holistic Sexuality

The Macro and Micro Lenses of Sexuality

As a writer, you understand the importance of moving between the different aspects of your story. A paragraph, to a scene, to a chapter, to the overall story. You learn how all those things work together. It's the same with sexuality. You need to have a mechanism to see all the different parts at different times. One aspect of the story movement, as I have discussed, is you. Let me introduce holistic sexuality.

If you understand the big sexuality picture, it helps you work the close-up sexuality picture. The big picture, or macro lens, starts with definitions; the detail, or micro lens, will be used to see your characters' physical, emotional, mental, and spiritual (PEMS) embodiment of sex.

The Macro Lens Position: The World

Below is the definition of sexuality provided by the World Health Organization (WHO), because "sexual health cannot be defined, understood or made operational without a broad consideration of sexuality, which underlies important behaviors and outcomes related to sexual health" (WHO, n.d.). I am using a macro definition—the world level—because most Americans have not dissected sexuality in these terms in their everyday life. If you choose to unpack the definition, the world that will be opened up to you is vast and detailed, and allows you to tap into not just knowledge, but empathy.

> A central aspect of being human throughout life encompasses sex, gender identities and roles, sexual orientation, eroticism, pleasure, intimacy and reproduction. Sexuality is experienced and expressed in thoughts, fantasies, desires, beliefs, attitudes, values, behaviors, practices, roles, and relationships. While sexuality can include all of these dimensions, not all of them are always

experienced or expressed. Sexuality is influenced by the interaction of biological, psychological, social, economic, political, cultural, legal, historical, religious and spiritual factors. (WHO 2015)

Sexual health is defined as

a state of physical, emotional, mental and social well-being in relation to sexuality; it is not merely the absence of disease, dysfunction, or infirmity. Sexual health requires a positive and respectful approach to sexuality and sexual relationships, as well as the possibility of having pleasurable and safe sexual experiences, free of coercion, discrimination and violence. For sexual health to be attained and maintained, the sexual rights of all persons must be respected, protected and fulfilled. (WHO 2015)

Unpacking the Definitions

- How do you actually apply these definitions?

- What do these look like in real life?

- How would you know a sexually healthy person or character if you saw them?

For writers, it's about showing.

If you check out "Life Behaviors of a Sexually Healthy Adult" on page 16 in *Guidelines for Comprehensive Sexuality Education* (SIECUS 2004), you will get some answers:

Link: https://qr1.be/X9TE   https://siecus.org/resources/the-guidelines/.

That list of behaviors is a starting point for you to measure your characters' behaviors against an outcome. There, you will get an idea of what the embodiment of sexuality and sexual

ASSESSMENT OF SEXUAL HEALTH, PART 1

Elements of Sexuality

health looks like in behavioral form. It will help you craft your narrative arcs, story-wise and sexuality-wise.

The Micro Lens Position: The Individual and PEMS Sexual Intimacy

Sexual information lives within you and your characters in your and their individual PEMS memory banks of the body. You experience the world in four dimensions of your body. While the physical dimension houses the other three components, you have your tactile nature to gather data and map your world. The same is true for emotions experienced, thoughts and beliefs processed, and your search for the meaning of it all on a grander scale. Each dimension can also be viewed as a macro component with details that you can break apart into micro components. And it is all history and material you can use as access to new content.

When you interact with others, you add those experiences—the collected data—to each dimension. When you choose to share intimately with a partner, that experience gets added, too. The depth in meaning builds.

These four PEMS places are also where you manage your Self to clarify where you and your characters stop and start. You pick what you will bring forward from yourself to be a part of your story and your characters. This may include information you didn't know was available, and once it is, you have it as material. I suggest that you use your personal, universal **emotions** for your character writing. Make a bank of them so you know where to go.

When you understand the broad nature of sexuality, with all its components, you can move into the micro portion of the characters and look at life behaviors. How will you bring forward their sexualities in a scene? What will give the reader the clearest sense of who they are? In Session 5, you will see how to take the sex history of a character's timeline and choose what will be most impactful for your story.

For now, you have tools to work on your story from macro and micro levels. Are there events from the sex history of your character which echo their overall motivation, so when you present them scene-wise, they match story-wise? More detail will be shared on sex history in Session 5, but I've listed two examples below of how you could sort through a sexual topic for your character using PEMS intimacy.

Example 1: Accidental Discovery of Masturbation in Childhood Bed

- **Physical:** Inadvertent. There was an itch in the vulva. Rubbing the area changed from itch to something pleasant. Exploration of the physical and good feelings occurred.

- **Emotional:** Excited. Secretive.

- **Mental:** When a boyfriend fantasy popped into the character's head, the sensations grew.

- **Spiritual:** "Am I the only one who has discovered this?"

If you get the specific details of any sex history event, you can choose which memories would fit best in your scene. This is how to access the information of the character.

Example 2: An Untimely Erection During a Book Report in Seventh-Grade English Class

- **Physical:** Erection. Blush. Increased heart rate. (Did you know that the body response to fear and arousal are similar?)

- **Emotion:** Fear, mortification.

- **Mental:** "Think of something else. Make it stop."

- **Spiritual:** "Why me? Why now?"

What Elements Might Change These Examples?

Consider what elements or other events might impact these events—other situations that could have previously occurred which would change the current experience.

For example, what if the character's sexual history includes confidence in walking around with no clothes? Maybe they grew up in a nudist camp, or their family skinny-dipped every summer; "naked" does not equal "sex," they have no negative baggage, and they are not ashamed of bodies or exploration. If you take the past sex history event apart and identify the elements of sexuality, you have another layer of character building with which to work.

Conclusion

PEMS, the physical, emotional, mental, and spiritual components, are wonderful repositories of a person's life. Knowing the specifics allows you to craft stories that pull the reader in. You can ask: Which aspect of PEMS is housed at the center of the character's sexuality? How does the context matter? This knowledge keeps you fully in the driver's seat of the story.

Session 4   Framing Your Sexuality Message with the PLISSIT Model

It All Started with Adam and Eve-The Company

My sexuality career had humble beginnings in North Carolina. The foundation for my three academic degrees sits squarely on the job I accepted after I dropped out of college. It was with Adam and Eve, where I packed a lot of condoms for customers. I was living in an applied sexuality model and I didn't even know it.

Phil Harvey, the founder of Adam and Eve, created the business as a result of his master's thesis in family planning from the University of Carolina at Chapel Hill. As I look back now, he was a staunch champion of sexual rights. This extended to philanthropy through DKT International, which provides condoms and birth control to people in Africa, Asia, and Latin America to eliminate the spread of STIs and promote family planning.

With this work experience under my belt, I knew my path and the focus of my education would be sexuality. Each degree provided another layer to my understanding and learning. During my first health education degree and my first professional job after my degree, I learned about the **PLISSIT model**, a framework for layering and discussing sexuality within the specific context of your audience:

- Are you setting a tone of **P**ermission when you talk?
- Are you helping to get rid of myths and misinformation and replace them with **L**imited **I**nformation facts?

- Are you providing resources—**S**pecific **S**uggestions related to the concerns in front of you?

- If these three levels don't address the concern, you move to **I**ntensive **T**herapy.

This was the first sexuality model I learned and is one I still use today. Jack Annon (1976) created this model for delivering sexuality information to psychology clients. Many have adapted this model and molded it to fit other areas where the delivery of sexuality information occurs.

While I first used the PLISSIT model with all its components in therapy, I readily adapted it to teaching and education. And now, I find it well-suited to discuss how to write sex.

Personal PEMS and the First Job

My work with Phil Harvey began March 1, 1977, and that date is a point on my sex history timeline. Let's apply PEMS before I go deeper into the PLISSIT model. Assessing with PEMS first provides me with the holistic balance of sexuality as I dig deeper into the PLISSIT details.

- **Physical:** A warehouse in Carrboro, NC. It housed people who dressed casually and moved around each other, working with a sexual ease.

- **Emotional:** Every day contained curious sexual topics, products, and conversations. I was excited, happy, and fulfilled, but I remained cautious about sharing where I worked.

- **Mental:** I noted the cognitive dissonance that arose when leaving the location and how people saw Adam and Eve differently than I did. I worked on how I thought about the conservative area where I lived. I thought through going back to get a health education degree. I read a course catalog and imagined how I could apply all the different areas of classes to my sexuality learning process at work. I considered philosophical, moral, and religious aspects of sexuality.

- **Spiritual:** Serendipity. "Am I being called to do this? Do I have the strength of character to keep going down this sexuality path?"

The PLISSIT Model: Adaptation for Sexuality Writing

I see the PLISSIT template as a living thing. You can move in and out of the first three parts every day and in any place. For your writing purposes, you will focus on the meaning of the first three elements.

The model rationale is to employ a writing style that allows for sexuality information to be freely disseminated and experienced while respecting and valuing the unique sexualities of characters. Here are the basics of the full model.

P: Permission

Permission involves you, the author, creating an environment where sexuality is permitted to be discussed in a respectful and thoughtful manner. This occurs at three levels.

First, you can create this element between your characters.

Second, you can create this element between you (the author) and your reader. The writer proactively meets the reader where they are and provides reassurances that sexuality content is normative. You set the stage for continued discussion and questions. The Self of the Writer is an important tool in the sexuality education process. Modeling an attitude of comfort with the topic is crucial. Use of a sensitive, nonjudgmental, and matter-of-fact style of discussion is essential.

This behavior by the author sets the tone of permission: You have permission to discuss sexuality. You have permission to embrace and enjoy your sexuality.

Third, you can provide information to other authors about how sexuality can be addressed in writing—information that shows you are a catalyst for a new paradigm.

It's possible that you may have already discovered this in your writing along the way. Maybe you sensed it. Now you can have the words to discuss what it is you are doing.

LI: Limited Information

Limited information occurs when one provides factual information on any sexuality topic of interest to a person.

This also involves clarifying misinformation and dispelling myths. It certainly means that you are not bringing misinformation forward.

When you offer new information or concepts, providing them in the context of life is important. Here are some examples.

- A character with a vulva might have difficulty with orgasm, so clitoral stimulation could be discussed.

- One character might think that all gay men have anal sex, so the idea of a side (a person who is not interested in anal sex) can be introduced. Sex without penetration is still sex. ("Guys on the 'Side': Looking beyond Gay Tops and Bottoms" 2013)

- Perhaps you want to show a character having sexual agency, a concept that includes the decision making and boundary clarity.

- A character poses "Am I normal?" This sets up a situation to discuss what is normal sexually?

These are but a tiny example of how limited information in sex writing could be addressed. It is dependent on your story, your characters and where the characters are in their journey.

SS: Specific Suggestions

The next component is to identify specific suggestions directly related to a human-sexuality topic. To do this well you need to identify sources. If you look at the examples in Limited Information, you may suggest a specific book, professional, website, or organization to tie to the specific topic you are presenting.

As you write, when a character has a specific concern, you can position other characters to provide the needed specific information. One character might have a sex-negative viewpoint, and another character counters with a sex-positive viewpoint. This is an example of how you can demonstrate each side of the sexuality coin.

IT: Intensive Therapy

The final component, intensive therapy, involves a referral to a sexuality professional (licensed and/or nationally certified) for private, confidential, individualized therapy when more specialized or detailed sexual interests and concerns must be addressed.

It's possible that you will write about a sexuality situation in your story that resonates emotionally and/or jars the reader. In that case, you could always list resources for further investigation. For example, in case someone wants to talk with a therapist, you could list the American Association of Sexuality Educators, Counselors, and Therapists, which has a referral network for all three positions in seven different countries: https://www.aasect.org/referral-directory.

How to Use PLISSIT in Your Writing

When you write, you create a tone or attitude through your writing style. That's where permission resides. You may do this through one character providing the permission for another character. One character may understand that something specific is bothering another character, and so you set up a fictionally realistic portrayal of them discussing specific suggestions. If you are looking for emotional glue for your characters, ask, Are they nervous? Are they happy someone noticed? How have you addressed those emotions?

Maybe you identify the specific character who will share limited information here. When you know your theme, your characters' sex history, and their PEMS material, you are positioned to add roles or aspects of personality in a fictionally realistic way as you layer in sexual details for them.

If you also employ the holistic components of sexuality, PEMS, you have a way to assess your approach in your story and scene. Using the structure of the PLISSIT model overlaying PEMS, you show your abilities as an author to be sex-positive and hold on to a larger perspective for character development and setting. Think of it as an invitation to the characters and the readers to sit with you and feel okay about sexuality. It also gives you solid ground to discuss the why and how of what you are weaving together in your tapestry.

Adding the PEMS Layer: Elements to Consider

Physical

How do you describe bodies? Is it shaming? Or something else? Do you use internalization to embellish what the physical body is experiencing? To highlight it? In the physical world, do characters use condoms, lube, sex toys? All of this is framing, and you are adding it as it fits into the character's world.

SEXUAL EVENT PEMS REFLECTION

Sexual Event

P: Physical

E: Emotional

M: Mental

S: Spiritual

Reflection

Emotional

What is the character feeling in relation to sexuality at the moment? What is that feeling tied to? Sex history? Relationship history? Knowing this helps us connect with the character. You create empathy for the character with these sensations and true feelings about what happened to them. You are including the past, present, and future in your work—multidimensional and multifaceted. This allows for the characters' complexities.

Mental

What kind of self-talk does the character have? Which side of the sexuality coin are you presenting? If it's the negative side, is that to provide a holistic picture that will shift, or is it a potential author intrusion? How can you use both sides of the coin to balance the character information on the topic?

Spiritual

What is the higher meaning of sex for the character? What realm do they filter their life through? Is it a specific religion about which they are working through ideas and/or changes for themselves? Are they more universal with spirituality rather than naming a specific religion? Do they use a personal code rather than a religious construct? Perhaps they created their own system and live by that.

Takeaways

The choices, the feelings, the thinking, and the application of the meaning sit in everything the character does sexually. When you write the layers of PEMS, you bring forward a way to better connect us to the character, allowing us to experience their plight, and perhaps even causing us to question your own. When you fold PLISSIT over the holistic model, you create a full world of the character.

Good writing does that, right?

As you read, you apply writing to yourself or compare it to your situation in life. Given that writing is important to you as a reader, you as the author can appreciate the reality that how you choose to present your writing is a teaching arena in sexuality. When you are in that arena, it has the capability to rewire your brain and change the old information you had. It really is an unconscious process that you work on within storytelling.

I want to remain an advocate of balancing sexuality and using it more intentionally to help us all continue on our journeys, as writers and humans. By now, I hope you know it's macro and micro.

There is your personal journey.

There is your author journey.

There is your character journey.

You are living this model.

Now perhaps, it's with frameworks, templates and a new thinking process.

KNOW YOUR CHARACTERS

Session 5   Sex History of Your Characters

The Next Layer

Most people go into writing sex feeling inadequate. You may have no frame of reference and no real starting point. Let's go to your character bible.

If you don't know, a character bible is an outline filled with everything there is to know about a character: their history, personality, motivations, and desires. When I first researched this, I couldn't find anyone who had added sexuality as a component, and yet it is a part of who people are. It makes us whole.

Giving characters a sex history provides you with content and context for setting up their sex in scene. You can be clear about how they will speak about sex and their attitudes toward sex. The characters embody all of these elements that are from their life experiences to date.

Before you read this material, did you think about your characters holistically—including sex? I bet you can tell me everything about them except what they have done sexually. You have been culturally trained to eliminate sex in your own life, so why would you think to add it to a character? When you have not received permission to focus on sex, it is hard to maintain. Well, here it is. I give you permission. You need to know everything about your character. So, let's layer in the sexual history.

Sex-Negative and Sex-Positive

Consider this: Sexual experiences mold people. Generally, I have found that people are influenced positively or negatively. No one is neutral on the topic. How might this influence manifest?

Example 1: Two Characters Going on a Date

- **Character A:** Grew up in Sweden.

- **Character B:** Grew up in Appalachian Mountains.

How would these two people even get together?

What is one possibility? A foreign exchange student comes to town.

Their meeting becomes a data point on each character's sexual history timeline.

When do exchange programs happen in the US? Usually high school. This provides a frame of reference for development. Age. Place. Education.

What might a sexual encounter between these two be like? Is it a sexual debut? Notice my language. I did not frame these characters as virgins. Remember to have progressive thinking and be sex-positive.

Example 2: Two Characters Going on a Date

- **Character C:** First job was a cook at a nudist colony.

- **Character D:** First job was writing anti-sexuality ads.

How would these two people even get together?

One possibility is that each character just moved to the same city and are next-door neighbors who share a back porch.

Their meeting becomes a data point on each character's sexual history timeline.

They are launching into the world. Age. Place. Education.

What might a sexual encounter between these two be like? What information would you need to have in order to explain how, when, where, and why this would occur?

If you are like many writers, the information you need in order to flesh out these examples lives in the character bible. You are creating multidimensional characters that you are sharing with the reader. But if you haven't had permission or been taught to include sexuality, you may not have had factual material to draw on.

Reflection

Now, press your personal life-pause button. I want you to stop and assess what automatically occurred to you with the first two examples.

Ask yourself: How did I conceptualize or visualize these characters?

- **Physical:** Male–male, male–female, female–female, female–nonbinary, etc.?

- **Emotional:** Were they stereotyped in how they display emotions?

- **Mental:** Were their thinking processes created through gender stereotypes or was gender identity even taken into account?

- **Spiritual:** What about their values, ethics, or ways of seeing the world through their sexuality? How did those elements play into your thoughts?

This is a great place to stop and check your biases about your characters. You will be better prepared to provide the details to give us rich characters.

CHARACTER PLANNING WITH SEXUALITY

Physical Description and Ability	Basic Information
	(Name, age, pronouns, race, etc.)

Family	Culture and Ethnicity

Class and Education	Location and Region

Values and Ethics	Religion

Motivations and Desires	Emotions
	(Honored? Numbed? Regulated? Stereotyped?)

Personality	Mental State and Ability
	(Neurodivergent? Trauma? Learning disability?)

Gender and Sexuality	
Gender and sexuality can be influenced by all previous categories. Has the character been positively or negatively influenced? Valid? Stereotyped?	

Use your macro and micro lens.

Use your PLISSIT template.

Clarify the boundaries between the author and characters.

Put yourself in action for your characters and your story.

Create a Character Sexuality Timeline

How can you get more information about the four people in the examples? Investigating their life and asking them questions. Let's set that up.

Your tool is to create a guiding timeline of sexual things that happened for each character *as they grew up*, from birth to the age they are now. It's called a character's **sex history**, and you will use their life stages from their development.

It's normative, and it will help you frame any scene with the sex you want.

The sex continuum for your timeline can be varied in activity and experience.

The extent to which your individual characters are sexually wise in your story can vary from character to character. When the differences are large, you can find conflict. But the important part is making the two (or more) characters fit as people in their motivations, needs, and wants. Find the places where they mesh. Find the places where they can help each other overcome obstacles. You can accomplish this through the situations you put them in, their internal conflicts, and their wants and needs.

What you may find helpful and interesting is writing up your *own* timeline, from birth to this moment. If you can do this for the one person you know well, it will be easier to create it for your characters. It's the bonus of working the Self of the Writer. It will become clear if you are unconsciously putting aspects of yourself in the character, or if you are using just the emotions that you experienced to enrich the characters you are introducing to us. If you do this, you will add to your detailed-writing repertoire.

Start Developing Your Characters' Sexual History

Consider your story as a piece of music. You are in the studio laying down the tracks to your song (the layers of your character). Sexuality is one of those tracks. It might be a specific instrument and it changes throughout your story. It has a beginning, a middle, and an end in the song and your story.

In realistic fiction, the beginning might involve childhood sexuality; the middle, the formative years of high school and then work or college. The end is where the character is in the story now. Look at how you can use that information in your story.

You can also consider your story as a tapestry. You are laying down the colorful threads on the structural frame—threads which you will weave into a colorful fabric, representing different aspects of your character spread across the story. Now consider sexuality the purple strand. Just like the other threads, it is already there for you to pick up and pull along with the character for the moments it's needed.

The layers you create for your character are incomplete if you've left out their sexual history. Most folks don't think about this because they haven't been taught to think about their own. The content you obtain about the character helps you with their wants and needs in the story, but also helps you develop and create rich characters.

Life Development Stages

Life development stages are formative events for the character as their personality develops. They include:

- **Prenatal development:** Your family origin story and what it means to your family. You are biologically identified as female, male, or intersex.

- **Infancy and toddlerhood:** You become attached with affection or isolated and lonely.

- **Early childhood:** You receive negative or positive messages about body image and body functions, including toileting.

- **Middle childhood:** You begin to formulate who you are concerning your identity, including sexual Self.

- **Adolescence:** You respond to Self and others about sexual body changes related to growing toward adulthood.

- **Early adulthood:** You begin independent expression of your sexual Self in the world.

- **Middle adulthood:** You balance your sexual Self within relationships and over time.

- **Late adulthood:** You consider what you haven't done with sexuality, and you do it before you die (Mcleod 2023).

Now consider those events compared to the learning components for psychosocial growth as outlined by Erik Erikson. He believed that personality is shaped over the life span, which implies that experiences later in life can heal or improve problems in early childhood. He believed you can negotiate conflict in relationships. Your human development happens in relation to other people, psychological and social. Sexuality is in all of it. Here are Erikson's life stages:

- **Trust vs. Mistrust:** Year 1.

- **Autonomy vs. Shame and Doubt:** Toddlerhood.

- **Initiative vs. Guilt:** Ages 3–5.

- **Industry vs. Inferiority:** Ages 6–11.

- **Identity vs. Role Confusion:** Teenage years; formation of identity.

- **Intimacy vs. Isolation:** Ages 19–40 (Mcleod 2023).

Here is a side-by-side comparison of the two frameworks based on Saul Mcleod's (2023) *Simply Psychology* article:

Stage	Basic Conflict	Activity	Virtue
Infancy (Birth To 18 Months)	Trust Vs. Mistrust	Feeding	Hope
Early Childhood (2 To 3 Years)	Autonomy Vs. Shame and Doubt	Toilet Training	Will
Preschool (3 To 5 Years)	Initiative Vs. Guilt	Exploration	Purpose
School Age (6 To 11 Years)	Industry Vs. Inferiority	School	Confidence
Adolescence (12 To 18 Years)	Identity Vs. Role Confusion	Social Relationships	Fidelity
Young Adulthood (19 To 40 Years)	Intimacy Vs. Isolation	Relationships	Love
Middle Adulthood (40 To 65 Years)	Generativity Vs. Stagnation	Work And Parenthood	Care
Maturity (65 To Death)	Ego Integrity Vs. Despair	Reflection On Life	Wisdom

Go through the stages. When parents have children, they live through what they haven't mastered for themselves; they get another opportunity. Hopefully, they don't instill their unresolved growth into their children, but many do. This is information that can help you create the obstacles to your character's journey.

Having a structure like this to guide you will be helpful in understanding your characters' growth in their respective development arcs.

Activity: Movie

Watch the movie, *How to Fall in Love*. Here are two trailers to get you started:

- https://www.hallmarkdrama.com/how-to-fall-in-love
- https://www.youtube.com/watch?v=1BGCfuP4c3I

When you watch the movie, pay attention to how one point on the hero's sexuality timeline shaped the hero's persona in the present time of the movie. The storytelling identifies the pivotal place and event where everything changed for Harold White with regard to his sexuality and how Annie Hayes was tied to it. The inclusion of the event highlights emotion and the trajectory change it caused in the character. Since the event occurred in adolescence, you could track its influence through the hero's stages of development.

How Do You Organize Sexual History?

First, this can be a two-part assessment: one for you and one for your character. Second, you can file sexuality information into the areas below and then organize them into the stages of life.

Area 1: Family Background

Describe the path your or your character's family has taken and the quality of the relationships that exist between various family members. It might show patterns.

Area 2: Explore Messages

Consider messages received in early life. These are the sexual scripts that people live by. How do those fit with your character's beliefs and attitudes of today? Your beliefs and attitudes?

Area 3: Explore Early Sexual Experiences

Explore your character's memories of masturbation and sexual interactions with other people. Explore how your character felt about the experiences they had and how the experiences shaped the way they now express themself sexually. Did your character have experiences that were coercive or nonconsensual? How did your character process these experiences, and how have they affected your character's sexuality? Does your character have significant relationships? What is your character's history with intimacy and sex? Has your character experienced a relationship the way they want to? Now ask each question about your own memories.

Area 4: Explore Sexual Orientation and Identity

What is or was your character's journey with gender identity and sexual orientation? What is or was your character's experience of Self on the male–female-nonbinary continuum? Your character's sexual experiences with same-sex partners and/or partners of other sexes can shed light on how sexuality is experienced and expressed in the present time of your story. In the journey, is your character carrying confusion, shame, or self-rejection that could affect their well-being? Now, what is or has been your journey with gender identity and sexual orientation?

Area 5: Identify Medical Issues and Overall Medical History

Some medical conditions apply to sexual history and functioning. Identify physical conditions and whether there are illnesses or issues that affect your character's sexual expression. Are they taking prescribed medications, using alcohol, or using drugs? Are there mental health concerns that might affect relationships and sexual expression? And what medical conditions apply to your sexual history and functioning?

Understanding of PEMS and your/your character's relational and sexual story gives you access to the experiences that influence character issues and their approaches to addressing them.

SEX HISTORY INTERVIEW, PART 1

Learning about Sex: Overall
Answer the following questions on learning about sex overall for yourself or a character.

How did you learn about sex/sexuality? From whom? (For example, parents, caregivers, siblings, friends, school, media, internet, religion, spirituality)

What age were you?

What did you learn from parents or caregivers? Which subjects were covered? (For example, pregnancy, birth, intercourse, menstruation, nocturnal emission, masturbation)

Was the information accurate? What was your reaction? How did you feel?

What did you learn from books, magazines, friends, or school?

Was the information accurate? What was your reaction? How did you feel?

What did you learn from personal experience?

How did your culture, ethnicity, or family background influence your attitudes about sex/sexuality?

What is the meaning/purpose of sex for you?

The Fiction Writer's Sexuality Guide ©2024 | author.com

Worksheet to Interview Characters on Sex History

Rounding Out Your Character

Questions help you get a new perspective about your character's sexuality. They provide a basis for portraying your character through their sexual development, reproductive health, interpersonal relationships, affection, intimacy, body image, and gender construction (SIECUS 2004.).

They are also a way to separate yourself from the character. If you, the author, answer these questions for yourself, you gain clarity in where your personal boundary as an author starts and stops, and the same is true for the characters you create. If you lay the answers out for your character, you will see a different developmental path that belongs totally to the character.

Answering these questions gives the character backstory for the reasons they do what they do today. Rather than keeping their sexuality on the shelf, you can take it, integrate it back into them, and then use the holistic nature of sexuality to make a fully formed, nuanced, and complex character. Remember, you don't have to show every single thing about the character, but you, the author, can have all the character information at your fingertips.

Consider the following events in story form:

Partners → practices → protection from STIs → history of STIs → prevention of pregnancy → accidents → yearnings → pain of loss → elation at surprises.

Take these elements, people, behaviors, experiences and feelings, and create a narrative, a story of "what happened." This is an example of a personal sex history. Pick a character and create how these things molded who they are in the present moment. You can do this for a character you've created in a story. This type of process allows you to provide sexuality details that make them who they are. You either hold them in your head, or share with the reader.

What is the emotion the character is feeling? How will you use that emotion while layering in backstory as you go along?

How significant was the event? The real and raw emotion? Was it a huge wallop like the pivotal event for the character in the movie *How to Fall in Love*? That event changed his life.

Chart Your Character

Once you've interviewed your character, the next step is creating a character timeline, or going back to the timeline you may have started in the Create a Character Sexuality Timeline section. It depicts their life from birth to their current age in the story. Place significant events on the timeline related to sex and sexuality.

The character answers the question, "What are the most important events in your life that shaped who you are sexually?" Think of this as a road map to where they are today. Plot each point on the journey. Fill up the page.

While you do experience life in this linear direction, it never feels like a straight line. Start with the developmental stages. Note the developmental stage the character is in when the event happens. What are the implications of it occurring in that time frame?

Add a different component by drawing it out as a road map through life. Draw this in an up-and-down movement.

Make each event a pin on the character's personal map. Most impactful sexual events, most impactful relationship events, turning points that shaped attitudes and beliefs. Have fun with learning your character.

Use the worksheet to help you stay focused on the meaning of the time frame in which the events and information occurred and how that can help you understand the character's current situation.

Sexual History Conclusion

You may have never considered sexual history in the way I presented here, but I bet you can see the value of this way now. Through sex, you can understand your characters. If you keep working to have that clarity for yourself as a writer, then creating holistic characters will be a breeze.

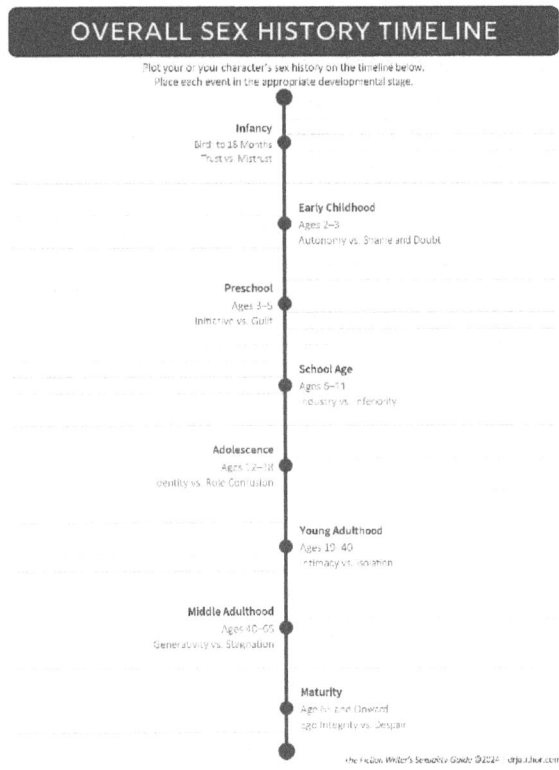

OVERALL SEX HISTORY TIMELINE

Plot your or your character's sex history on the timeline below.
Place each event in the appropriate developmental stage.

Infancy
Birth to 18 Months
Trust vs. Mistrust

Early Childhood
Ages 2–3
Autonomy vs. Shame and Doubt

Preschool
Ages 3–5
Initiative vs. Guilt

School Age
Ages 6–11
Industry vs. Inferiority

Adolescence
Ages 12–18
Identity vs. Role Confusion

Young Adulthood
Ages 19–40
Intimacy vs. Isolation

Middle Adulthood
Ages 40–65
Generativity vs. Stagnation

Maturity
Age 65 and Onward
Ego Integrity vs. Despair

Session 6   Writing Sexual Fantasies

Research on Fantasies

Since writing scenes with sex in the fiction world is the focus of the book, I want to include research about the fantasy life of individuals. To be clear, I mean what people do in their heads.

This is the M of PEMS, and many people want to keep it there. Fantasy is the private material that adds fuel for desire and arousal. Knowing this could help you conceptualize how your characters think about sex, or places for characters to come together, or places to create tension between characters. It speaks to solo sex, partner sex, and group sex.

Let's define a **sexual fantasy** as any mental picture that comes to mind while you're awake that turns you on. This is a conscious thought making you hot and bothered. For clarity, sleeping dreams are unconscious and fantasies are conscious, so they can't be compared.

Justin Lehmiller (2020) presents his research on sexual fantasy in his book *Tell Me What You Want: The Science of Sexual Desire and How It Can Improve Your Sex Life*. From his work, he identified seven themes of fantasy.

Study Background

What is impressive about this comprehensive study is that the participants wrote in their own words. Specifically, they wrote out their all-time favorite sexual fantasy in narrative form and also summed up the main idea of the fantasy in a word. After that, they completed follow-up questions about the who, what, when, and where of the fantasy (6).

Description of Participants

There were 4,175 participants from the US with a median age of thirty-two. There was a fifty–fifty split between those who indicated they were cisgender men and cisgender women. (7). They identified themselves as "heterosexual (72 percent), bisexual (12.6 percent), gay/ lesbian (5.7) percent), pansexual (4.2 percent), and queer (2.3 percent)" and this matches other national surveys where one third of the adults under the age of thirty said they are not completely heterosexual (8).

Leanings

People willing to discuss sex had positive views of sexual fantasies and reporting on their sex lives. Religious folks and republicans were underrepresented.

It is important to note that the demographics were not strictly representative of the US population, but it is nevertheless the largest and most diverse group of Americans to have reported on sexual fantasies. Many other sex research studies use college populations (9).

Lehmiller discusses the question, what is a normal fantasy? Basically, one that a lot of other people are having. Whether it is healthy or appropriate to act on is a separate issue.

Lehmiller's Seven Fantasy Themes

The all-time favorite sexual fantasies described by participants revealed seven categories considered as normal:

1. Multi-partner Sex

2. Power, Control, and Rough Sex (BDSM)

3. Novelty, Adventure, and Variety (Sexual Adventure)

4. Taboo and Forbidden Sex

5. Partner Sharing and Nonmonogamous Relationships

6. Passion and Romance

7. Erotic Flexibility (Homoeroticism and Gender-Bending) (11).

Highlight: Top Three Fantasies

Group Sex

The single most popular fantasy was group sex. The magic number for group sex was three. For cisgender men and cisgender women, *what* they did in the group sex fantasy was more important than the who and where. It could be a matter of sensory overload—amping arousal by having another body to look at, touch, and experience in an overpowering way so they get lost in sensations. This falls under the P of PEMS and the need for physical stimulation as identified in the Quantum Model put forward by David Schnarch, which will be addressed in Session 7.

Heterosexual men were more likely to prefer male–female–female (MFF) to female–male–male (FMM). Heterosexual women were more open to partners of the same gender and a same-sex threesome (14).

BDSM

The next most popular fantasy theme was **BDSM**, which stands for Bondage and Discipline, Dominance/submission, and Sadism and Masochism. These fantasies are about desires that evoke themes of power, control, and/or rough sex. A quarter of participants said a BDSM fantasy was their favorite fantasy of all time. Individuals who are not heterosexual were more inclined to have fantasies about BDSM, non-monogamous relationships, taboo behaviors, and activities involving changes in gender roles (106).

This is not to say that what you desire can't change across contexts. Someone who fantasizes about being dominant in one setting may fantasize about being submissive in other settings. It appears to depend on the partner and how the person fantasizing feels. In BDSM language, people who change it up are called switches.

B: Bondage is sex play in which someone takes pleasure in using physical restraints. One person surrenders control of their body to another. This allows them to be a sex object. More than three-quarters of participants reported they had bondage fantasies, and one-third of the group with bondage fantasies reported they had them often.

D: Discipline is sex play in which someone derives sexual arousal from the use of restraint, but psychological restraint. This is accomplished through the use of rules and punishment and is not quite as popular as bondage.

D/s: Dominance involves getting sexual pleasure from having power and control over someone else. **Submission** is receiving pleasure by ceding power and control to another. This can be physical, psychological, or both. Folks who enjoy D/s recognize that power comes with responsibility. Well-being is crucial. Perhaps frequent submission fantasies suggest the person doesn't want the responsibility that comes with control. Psychologically, being submissive changes you from a person to an object and helps take you out of your head.

S&M: Sadism and **masochism** are about getting sexual pleasure from giving and receiving pain. Spanking, biting, and whipping were the more commonly mentioned acts of S&M. The one giving pain is the sadist. The one receiving pain is called the masochist (19).

Themes of Novelty, Adventure, Variety

Novelty was based on the sexual activity. For example, some participants fantasized about engaging in oral pleasure or anal sex because they had never done those activities before or because they were imagining doing them in a new way. The adventure aspect focused on having sex in unique settings. Variety was about having unexpected, surprising, or thrilling sexual encounters, new directions. One in five participants identified novelties as their all-time favorite fantasy (28).

Conclusions for Writing

With Lehmiller's research, you have facts about what is going on in people's heads. This gives you material to use confidently. What are the stories individuals are creating for their own pleasure? This is something you can give your characters. Having a notion of what is considered normal in fantasy provides you with another aspect of character development to use.

With my therapist hat on, I ask, what makes this information stand out? You can use it for communication. This becomes an interesting source from which you can create the glue and intimacy of your characters. If they have fantasies, how do they share those interests? Are these events something they want to keep in their head? Would they like to talk about them as a sexual element in a scene? Could a discussion help a character talk clearly about what they want? You could track this as a sexual journey. Is there a recurring fantasy? Does it involve a partner?

You can use this knowledge as a writer to create the tension and reveal elements of sexual history. In real life, I've found that folks who want to go past vanilla sex and into activities providing more intensity work the language. They work with the clarity of consent. And they honor the other person or people in the relationship. Fantasy could be a specific area of sexual content that you can use to highlight character growth.

The Treasure Chest of Your Character's Sexual Mind

Consider using the science of fantasies to help you write. Over the course of your story, characters could introduce the idea of fantasy, instigate a discussion of fantasy, suggestion of a specific fantasy they like, read a fantasy during sexuality activities, all of which demonstrate degrees of sharing. And remember, fantasies can stay in your/character's heads, they do not need to come into real life acting out, but they could.

For your characters, you can use a fantasy as an element of a character's movement. It could be on their sexual history timeline.

For an element of tension between your characters, you could give them competing fantasies. Could it be an obstacle? Hidden information as a delightful surprise? Is a character fighting an internal battle about sharing the fantasy?

Now you can clearly label sexual elements that could drive your story in directions you may not have known about or considered. This is a top-down expansion by the author for the character.

Questions and Elements to Ponder

- Can the character be fantasizing while also participating in a (fictional) real-life encounter? Would this involve the character's partner knowing or not knowing?
- I like/dislike how my brain integrates a/my partner into the fantasy.
- I want my partner to participate with me in _____.
- What happens if the fantasy in the character's brain comes into their real life (in your fictional story)?
- What will communication be like between your characters on fantasy topics?
- How will they choose to respond?

Session 7 Motivations for Characters' Sex in Scene

Before delving into the motivations behind characters' sexual behavior in scenes, it's crucial to understand the concept of scene type and how it can assist you in your writing. **Scene type** refers to the writer's choice concerning the number of characters involved, their environment, and their activities. You will see the limits of scene combinations by examining these aspects.

For example, in scenes involving sex, you might have a solo character, a duo, a small group, a large group, or even a crowd. The setting could be indoors or outdoors, and the characters might be engaged in various activities like moving, being stationary, talking, working, playing, or interacting in different ways with strangers, friends, lovers, enemies, or their surroundings.

When selecting your scene types, be mindful to:

- Introduce unexpected elements.

- Reuse scene types in a manner that intensifies tension and leads the character to pivotal decision-making moments.

- Avoid overusing the same scene type consecutively. However, revisiting a scene type can be effective for reflecting or reinforcing a theme or idea at critical junctures in your narrative.

I find it useful to consider scene types within the framework of the MICE Quotient, as defined by Orson Scott Card in his book *Elements of Fiction Writing: Characters and Viewpoints* (Card, O.S. 1999). In this approach, a scene type is a fundamental component of all MICE stories.

What is a Mice Quotient?

Summary: Orson Scott Card's MICE quotient categorizes stories into four elements: Milieu, Idea, Character, and Event (62). In any narrative, while all four elements are present, Card suggests that one typically dominates. It's beneficial to identify which element is the primary focus in your story.

Milieu: A milieu story emphasizes the *world* or setting around the characters. It's about the environment, the cultural and social contexts in which the characters exist, including their culture, education, and social interactions. In such stories, the central theme is often a character's transition from one milieu to another, facing challenges to adapt or a desire to escape (62). With stories exploring sexual journeys, consider if the setting plays a specific role, like a unique "pleasure room" or a business linked to sexuality, adding a distinct sexual element to the narrative.

Idea: An idea story revolves around the critical *information* or insights the reader gains throughout the narrative, often started by a question (62). In narratives about sexual journeys, this question could be deeply connected to a character's sexual history. For instance, in the film "Good Luck to You, Leo Grande," the central question might be, "Can I find pleasure after an unfulfilling marital life?" The story then unfolds through the character's self-discovery.

Character: A character story focuses on the nature and development and motives of at least one main character. It starts with the character's dissatisfaction, leading to a change or acceptance by the end (62). The pivotal point in such stories is the character's dilemma, a choice between equally significant options, none of which are simple and all have substantial consequences.

A narrative focused on sexuality could center on a character undergoing significant personal transformation and facing critical choices regarding their sexual identity, relationships, or values. This could be, at any age, grappling with how they want sexuality to be different. It would follow a specific character's journey of self-discovery and the choices they make that drive the narrative.

Event: An event story is driven by significant happenings, particularly a catastrophic event that threatens the world—*what* happens and *why* it happens. The narrative progresses towards resolving, altering, or concluding with the outcomes of this event (62). A writer could focus on a significant event related to sexuality that has profound implications for the characters and the story. Here are a few examples of such an event:

- A new law or legal decision regarding sexual rights could be a central event.

- A new technology that alters sexual experiences could be an event—advanced virtual reality or a novel contraceptive method.

- A major cultural shift in attitudes about sexuality, like the sex revolution of the 1960s, could provide a rich backdrop for a character to become involved in these efforts.

Each of these scenarios offers a unique way to explore sexuality as a central event, driving the narrative and character development in profound ways.

Holding the concepts of milieu, idea, character, and event as components of sexuality gives you another tool to define and track its movement in your story.

Meaning of Sex in Scene

Your scene can drive any part of the MICE elements forward. In service to this, you can learn new ways to approach writing a scene with sex.

Diana Gabaldon (2016) says, "A good sex scene is dialogue with physical details. It's the exchange of emotion, not bodily fluids." This is supported by the *The Bestseller Code*, in which the authors comment on connection and human closeness. They identify that people communicating in moments of shared intimacy, shared chemistry, and shared bond is what the readers want to experience—the closeness of the characters (Archer and Jockers 2016, 67).

So, for a scene with sex, consider the idea of putting the physical in the background and the emotion in the foreground.

To clarify your scene, you must be clear on why your characters are having sex. This creates *meaning* for sex. And the meaning inspires the *type* of sex.

This is nuanced, but as you take apart the layers to create sex in a scene, you get skilled. Even if you are working to hit the beats of a genre or publish a specific item, consider the meaning of sex to the specific character.

Why Do People Have Sex?

Why do people have sex? Great question. And for writers, it is crucial to know the answer, as it relates to why you are putting it in your story. If you know the reason for your characters, then you know exactly why the scene with sex exists and will use it to show lots of information about the character.

My former boss used to say that people use sex as a multipurpose cleaner. It's a physical tool that expresses, soothes, and brings about many emotions. Happy. Sad. Grieving. Angry. Remorseful. Healing. Lonely. Tired. Anxious. Release. This means, if you identify the specific emotion—whatever emotion—you can use it as the embodiment of sex.

Case Study: Outlander

To bring these concepts alive, I want to give you a concrete example of the meaning of sex through visual storytelling and written storytelling. The example will be from the TV series *Outlander*, adapted from the novels by Diana Gabaldon.

First, the screenplay uses much of the dialogue from Gabaldon's novel. I believe this speaks volumes about how much the written dialogue contributes to the movement of the story.

Second, I watched an interview where *Outlander* actors Sam Heughan and Caitríona Balfe said they reread the book each season was based on before they began filming (Balfe et al. 2020). I also heard this from Wes Chatham, the actor who plays Amos on *The Expanse* series based on the books by James S. A. Corey (Chatham and Franck 2022). "I always read *The Churn* because it is the psychological foundation of the character Amos, how he is, who he is, the meaning (7:20). These actors were looking for the details about their character, past and present, and their emotional experiences in order to dive deeply into their role and tap into those emotions in themselves.

This is telling for writers. The emotion lives in the middle of the scene, like a river or a creek, depending on what you need. The reader needs to feel it and understand it and know what it is connected to.

I'm using *Outlander*'s episode "The Wedding" from Season 1 because there are three distinct types of sex in scene (Foerster and Moore 2014). Based on this alone, you can see that the context of the meaning of sex creates different scenes with sex.

The emotional set up to this episode occurs in the previous episode "The Garrison Commander" at the 54:58 minute (Kelly, Brian and Moore 2014). Look at this back-and-forth dialogue between characters Claire Beauchamp and Jamie Fraser before their wedding. The information in the eleven-word question and twelve-word answer sets the stage for tension, conflict, and much meaning for the three scenes with sex that follow after the wedding.

> Claire: "Well, doesn't it bother you that I'm not a virgin?"
>
> Jamie: "No. So long as it doesna bother you that I am."

Analyzing scenes from both the show and the books on which the show is based can be very telling about the writing process. Watch and read scenes with an author's eye.

Name the meaning behind each scene with sex. With the visual, watch the actors bring to life the emotion, motivation, and dialogue that relate to the sexual action.

Then, through a screenwriting position, look at all the dialogue and consider what physical components would highlight the words and the meaning behind the words, covert and overt, subtext or direct communication. It is all material, and it helps you get more from your scene with sex.

Discussion of *Outlander,* Season 1, Episode 7, and the Three Scenes with Sex

As I set the stage for this discussion, consider some basic information about these characters.

Jamie	Claire
• Values culture, clan, and religion. Law-abiding.	• Values come from a different century.
• Finds clothes, church, and ring for wedding.	• Thinking of already being married to Frank in front of a judge and being a bigamist.
• Wants to marry to make his mother proud.	• Thinks of herself as an adulterer and places Frank's ring in bodice.
• Values not sinning.	• Spends the wedding day drinking.

Note the motifs of oaths, bond, safety, loyalty, and consent, and how all have a different meaning and feeling for Jamie and Claire. Carry that with you into their scenes with sex.

Scene 1, 12:24: Legality, Consummation, Technical PinV Intercourse

> Claire: "It's getting rather late. Perhaps we should go to bed."
>
> Jamie: "To bed or to sleep?"
>
> Claire: "Well…"
>
> Jamie: "Either way you're not likely to sleep in your corset. I'll help you with the laces and such."
>
> [He holds out his hand. She accepts it. Undressing occurs. Note that Jamie begins sex from behind Claire, and she turns her body so they are face-to-face for the missionary sex position. Quick sex occurs.]

Consider what that means, that Claire changed positions. Also note that the quick sex matches the essence of this scene; it seals the marriage contract.

Scene 2, 39:39: Curiosity and Pleasure

In the beginning of this scene, Jamie is taking off his boots. He reflects on the wedding ceremony and the handfasting ritual. (This brings into focus the meaning the wedding had for him.) Jamie and Claire change position again. Who leads? Who orchestrates oral sex?

Claire: "What exactly did the words mean?"

Jamie: "You are blood of my blood, and bone of my bone. I give you my body that we two may be one. I give you my spirit 'til our life shall be done." [Kisses the bride.] "When you kissed me like that, well, maybe you weren't so sorry to be marrying me after all."

[Watch the movement from here: Claire strokes Jamie's arm. He looks expectant and then disappointed when Claire stands and walks across the room, but she turns.]

Claire: "Take off your shirt. I want to look at you."

[He removes the shirt. She places her hand to his chest. Claire walks around him, touching him. Faces him.]

Jamie: "Alright. Fair is fair. Take off yours as well." [Claire removes her gown. Jamie takes a step back.]

Claire: "Have you never seen a naked woman before?"

Jamie: "Aye, but not one so close. And not one that's mine."

[They kiss. Move onto the bed. Missionary. Loud moaning and groaning. Jamie thinks he has hurt Claire because of her response, which was to orgasm. Claire flips them and moves on top of Jamie. Now watch how the dialogue is positioned with the physical movements. Claire uses her teeth.]

Claire: "Do you want me to stop?

Jamie: "No."

[She gives Jamie oral sex; he has an orgasm and laughs.]

Jamie: "I thought my heart was going to burst."

The focal point is the emotion and thoughts showcasing different types of sex, revealing knowledge about sex, and adding tension to what the sex accomplishes for each of them.

Scene 3, 49:23: Heart, Tender Intimacy, Connection with Sex

Next, Jamie wakes up and sees Claire sitting in a chair. He gets pearls and drapes them over her head.

> Jamie: "They're Scotch pearls. They belonged to my mother. And now they belong to my wife. They are one of the few things I have left of her. Very precious to me, as are you, Claire."
>
> [She kisses his shoulder. Strokes his face and kisses him. Climbs on his lap. Deep gazing and touching. Claire wraps the wool around them in a cocoon and kisses him. Both lead and both follow. Actions are no longer tentative; they are connected and moving together.]

Think of a scene with sex as a situation that highlights, contrasts, and/or illuminates the wants and needs. It builds the story. It provides a lesson for the protagonist. The scene holds meaning in the story and in the character. The characters live these words: meaning, description, act, react. Consider the words in the scene. Dialogue gives us one perspective. What action matches the dialogue? What action is in contrast to it?

Also, consider using tango videos to study physical and emotional responses. Imagine the story in between each move. Internal dialogue. External movements. If you consider the physical activity of sex as a dance which is experienced by the dancer (character) with all their history, attitudes, and beliefs activated by a specific type of music (emotion) then you have a way to visualize and experience the dance (sex) from the minute it begins until it ends. You can imagine all the possible mixtures.

It's possible that one dancer is a more practiced dancer than the other. One might know many dances with varied music. Maybe one is more confident even though they don't know the steps. Maybe one is an eager learner.

It's the way you present the physical sex by layering in all these different elements that will make it zing for the reader. Remember, if you think of your Writer Self as a weaver and the writing as a tapestry, you have threads to anchor from the beginning. Sex needs a dedicated thread. MICE components help you find your threads.

Let me put my sex therapy hat on here and discuss one more element called the Quantum Model of Sex.

Quantum Model of Sex

Here is another component for how to look at the meaning of sex in scenes. David Schnarch (1991) created the theoretical **Quantum Model of Sex** and outlined it in his book, *Constructing the Sexual Crucible*. He writes, "At its most basic level, the quantum model is an economic model of genital functioning integrating physiological stimulation and intrapsychic processes. In its richest elaboration, it integrates intimacy, emotional meaning, and sexual potential" (22).

Schnarch used it to help clients see when they were or weren't getting the stimulation they needed to move through the sexual response cycle. To learn this information, key questions are: Can the individual reach the body reflex of arousal (erection or lubrication), and can the individual reach the body reflex of orgasm? For example, for people with vulvas, is there enough physical stimulation at the right time and the right place to reach arousal and/or orgasm? Conversely, for people with penises, is there too much stimulation so they are getting to orgasm faster than they want?

This model is helpful in that it adds another layer of potential tension and contrast, highlighting what each person needs to have going on in the brain to get rolling sexually. Schnarch addresses two sexual stimulation areas: physical stimulation (tactile, experiential) and psychological stimulation (thoughts, impressions, likes and needs). He notes people might get there with a combination of both, such as 70 percent physical and 30 percent psychological, or the converse, or any combination you can create, including 100 percent physical or 100 percent psychological. And since sex is individualistic, this information is helpful in considering responses from characters and how you use their sex history to amplify the physical and psychological components (24).

Knowing this information could help you craft your character's way of having sex—what they like and want—because you would know how their body works. Consider all the obstacles that could result because of different needs between characters.

However you've created the sex, when you have individuals moving forward physically and enjoying pleasure through their PEMS experience, when the people together have reached the moment of "we are on the same page," you cannot tell where each individual stops and starts. You cannot tell who is leading and who is following in the action-response pattern. When the in-sync moments occur, the whole sexual experience builds because of the emotion, desire, and yearning. The specific emotion drives the physical train.

This model also harkens back to the question, why? You need to understand the overarching why of the story and the why in the scene. The more you can tie these together, the richer the story will be.

Ask yourself, how do MICE components fit into my scene?

How does the dialogue add to the context?

How does the physical activity fit with meaning, needs, and wants?

Create this new template for yourself to frame your story on the macro and micro levels.

Taking a scene apart to observe the context gives you the space in which to craft. Again, it doesn't matter if you're a pantser or a plotter because once your scene is on the page, you can lay this template over it for edits and revision. You have so many elements to work with. Your issue will be asking, "Oh, where to start?" while rubbing your hands together and waggling your eyebrows, rather than wringing your hands, cringing, and saying, "Where do I start?"

Session 8   What Makes a Complete Relational Sexual System?

A Theoretical Perspective on Sex

I see lots of authors use different personality frameworks like Myers-Briggs or the Enneagram to create characters' internal makeups, so I want to add a sexual personality framework to the mix.

Let me introduce you to the **Crucible Model** by David Schnarch (1991).

This system which focuses on the Self within the relationship system identifies and uses emotions that can help you see how individuals grow within a partnership. It highlights how the relationships negotiate sex.

I think it fits well in writing because writers understand that their characters must go through obstacles to grow. The Crucible Model is a systemic approach to understanding where relationships get stuck, how to unstick them, and what growth looks like.

Schnarch found that a marriage or committed relationship can't succeed unless you claim your sense of Self in the presence of the other. That action and the resulting growth fuel the committed relationship and enable passionate sex. Claiming your sense of Self also pays wide-ranging dividends in other domains, from friendship to creativity to work.

Claim your Self through differentiation.

I learned about differentiation in my doctoral program studying Bowen Theory (Bowen 1978), Edwin Friedman's (Friedman 1990) use of it, and then Schnarch's (Schnarch 1991) conceptualization of their work.

Differentiation is the process of maintaining a distinct, individual identity while being emotionally connected to a partner. It involves resisting the pressure to conform to a partner's expectations and beliefs, particularly when the partner holds significant emotional importance in one's life. Schnarch emphasized that a balanced relationship is not about dependence or independence, but about interdependence. In such a relationship, both partners are emotionally self-sufficient, able to manage their own emotional needs while also supporting each other's goals and adapting to changing circumstances. Flexibility and a focus on strengths, contrasting with dependent relationships, where partners continuously compensate for each other's limitations and needs, characterizes this interdependent dynamic.

Conceptually similar to the biological process of differentiation, where cells become more distinct as they evolve, it can also be a psychological/emotional development. We can observe this when individuals move away from their family of origin and become more unique and specialized in psychological and emotional aspects.

Individuals frequently internalize their level of differentiation from their parents and family of origin. Children typically mirror or fall below their parents' levels of differentiation, but some, because of life experiences, therapy, or their partners, achieve a higher level of differentiation than their parents. And if we look at how characters in their sex history addressed or handled sexual concerns, differentiation or lack thereof sit there.

Relationships are Crucibles

David Schnarch's metaphor of a crucible vividly describes intimate, committed relationships as intense and transformative environments (Schnarch 1991, xv). A mix of conflict, gridlock, anger, pain, lust, love, desire, growth, and creativity characterizes these relationships.

He viewed them as essential for personal development and growth, with sexuality being an effective catalyst for self-improvement. More specifically, he considered sexuality the window into a couple/individual's state of adjustment, present-day life concerns, and unresolved emotional growth (Schnarch 191, 157).

Schnarch maintained that one's personal beliefs, preferences, and goals within a relationship are more challenging. Achieving differentiation in a relationship can extend to other areas of life, such as defending one's position at work or upholding principles under pressure.

Differentiation and Choosing a Partner

In relationships, differentiation balances two opposing forces:

- Attachment/Togetherness: The desire to be loved and belong, often leading to the minimization of personal preferences to gain a partner's love.

- Autonomy/Individuality: The desire to maintain one's identity, summarized as "this is who I am, take it or leave it."

Poorly differentiated individuals often find themselves dominated by one of these forces, leading to a dichotomy of either maintaining their identity or being close to others. Differentiation is the ability to balance autonomy with attachment, allowing for a connection to one's own thoughts, values, and feelings while being close to someone important. It can also be seen as being close while avoiding reactivity. When you are differentiated, you are independent and connected.

In the context of relationships, differentiation and the choice of a partner deeply intertwine. People generally lean towards one of two polarities - autonomy or attachment. This inclination influences their selection of partners, friends, colleagues, and even workplaces, typically attracting those with a similar level of differentiation and capacity for intimacy. The interplay of these preferences shapes the relationship's dynamic:

- Partners both leaning towards attachment often form a symbiotic relationship.

- Those favoring autonomy tend to have a volatile relationship, with both partners competing for dominance.

- The most common dynamic is a mix, with one partner inclined towards autonomy and the other towards attachment, often switching roles.

Poorly differentiated relationships exhibit several characteristics:

- Avoidance of conflict, with partners deeply entrenched in the attachment polarity, leading to a symbiotic dynamic.

- Constant fighting, where partners stuck in the autonomy polarity struggle to reconcile differences.

- Cutoffs, such as family members not communicating for extended periods, or children moving away to establish autonomy.

- High reactivity and emotional fusion, where partners' emotions trigger each other, leading to either emotional distance or constant conflict to cope with intimacy issues.

Schnarch also discusses two ways of experiencing the self: the reflected sense of self and the solid sense of self (Schnarch 1991, 203).

The reflected sense of self is relational and dependent on feedback from parents, family, and society. It is about other-validation. This perspective is predominant in childhood and adolescence, where external validation and avoidance of criticism shape self-perception. Operating from this sense of self leads to caution in self-revelation, as external feedback significantly impacts confidence and self-image.

Conversely, the solid sense of self represents a more mature self-awareness. It is characterized by a strong sense of personal identity, self-worth, and beliefs, regardless of external feedback, it is self-validation. This sense of self relies on the prefrontal cortex's ability to maintain personal convictions despite criticism and conflict. "In fact, self-discipline (in the form of differentiated functioning) is a key to intense levels of eroticism and intimacy (Schnarch 1991, 67)." Schnarch believed that integrity was at the heart of differentiation. "When you choose to use sexuality as a vehicle for self-discovery and you do it in front of a partner, you are working at the highest levels of personal integrity (Schnarch 1991, 158)."

Understanding how people form relationships based on the Self allows you to write with confidence about the conflict and connections in the relationship. The way an individual handles anxiety plays a crucial role in how they navigate the obstacles and crises presented in your story.

Thinking about sexuality as the window into the individual provides a deeper understanding of how individuals grow. I created a visual representation of the model and a way for you to place your characters in it.

The Idea of Differentiation

In *Constructing the Sexual Crucible*, Schnarch (1991) defines differentiation as:

1. The ability to maintain one's sense of separate self in close proximity to a partner

2. Non-reactivity to other people's reactivity

3. Self-regulation of emotionality so that judgment can be used

4. The ability to tolerate pain for growth (114)

An Approach to Physical Intimacy: Hugging and Kissing

Let's use hugging and kissing as ways to understand the embodiment of emotion. Depending on their levels of differentiation, people move their bodies in specific ways.

In both cases, I want you to consider how the approach is accomplished and what would make people go about kissing or hugging that way.

The Hug

Get ready to do visualization work. Consider two people hugging. From the side, do they look A-shaped, with the tops of their bodies touching but distance between their bottom halves? Are they

THE CYCLE OF SELF: MODEL

Event, Issue, or Concern

Anxiety

Attempts to Get Rid of Anxiety

Cut Off or Withdraw from Other

Take Over Other

Be Taken Over by Other

DIFFERENTIATE

1) Maintain sense of separate self; other close to another
2) Be nonreactive to other's reactivity
3) Self-regulate emotions so that judgment can be used
4) Tolerate this new uncomfortable feeling because it leads to growth

Get New Data

The Fiction Writer's Sexuality Guide ©2014 | drauthor.com

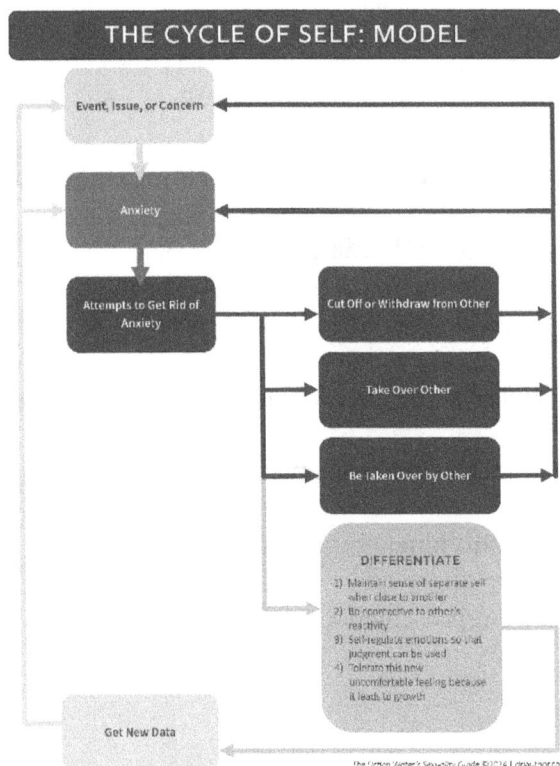

parallel, like two vertical lines of an H, and do they quickly step up to form the crossbar and step away? Are they comfortably close, or are they uncomfortably close? Is one more comfortable than the other? Does their level of comfort depend on who is doing the hugging and who is being approached? Does it depend on what the meaning of the hug is? From a movement standpoint, how do they go about it?

If you want to experience the emotion in this activity, ask for volunteers and watch what they do.

✍

Hugging Activity

Select two people to help you with hugging. Your words could be: "I'm working on a research piece for my novel, and I'm wondering if you could help me out. Can you show me how you hug? Or can you give each other a hug?"

Provide no more instructions. You will see how the intent, the meaning, and the emotion unfold in front of you. Note who starts the hug, who ends the hug, and how long it lasts. Now consider this in relation to differentiation. You will see a relational component in real time, and it's one that you can use in your writing.

Dr. Schnarch created an exercise he called "Hugging 'til Relaxed" (Schnarch 1993). Consider this question: Can you calm and quiet yourself with your arms wrapped around someone and their arms wrapped around you? It is an exercise of boundaries, the amount of Self, and holding emotions. Hugging can be a physical expression of and/or precursor to emotional connections that sit in the meaning of sex and the people who are experiencing their Selves. The more you can identify the nuances of emotional meaning and put them in physical descriptions, the less you will be just describing body parts; instead, you will be describing the reason the body parts are coming together in the way they are. Remember the adage, "Look at what people do rather than what they say." If you know the physical, you can go back and add in the meaning. If you know the meaning, you can create the physical.

The Kiss

Apply the same type of consideration to how someone kisses.

Is it a tight-lipped kiss, or an open-mouth kiss with lots of tongue? Does someone dive in or hang back? Does someone wait and let the other lead?

There are many aspects to kissing. The partners could be leisurely working all details around the mouth, savoring them as if there is all the time in the world, or there could be a let's-get-this-over-with feeling. Look at the duration of the kiss. Who pulls away and why? Watch any romance movie or movie with a relationship arc and look at the way kisses are set up. Check out who led and who followed and dilemmas created.

These are simple ways to get more from the physical embodiment of sex, and the two activities can help you set up your scenes and provide the specific context of emotion and sex for your characters.

Consensual Nonmonogamy

Not all relationships are monogamous. One in six North American adults participates in polyamory, one type of consensual nonmonogamy (CNM) (Kinsey, 2022).

Keeping an open mind to showcase characters diverse in the ways they think and live will serve a broader audience and the goal of education.

When writing, you may choose to create new family groupings. For example, consider those that involve a loving component, as in polyamory or ethical nonmonogamy, where characters would have to negotiate specific details with their partners on how their relationship will work. No matter what, you may find yourself wondering how to put a CNM grouping together in a fashion that makes sense for your story and your characters' development.

Lehmiller (2021) identified six reasons people want CNM relationships:

- **Autonomy.** It feels like a natural and authentic fit for the person.

- **Belief Systems.** Two ideas: Open relationships give you more opportunities to learn and grow, and it makes sense not to have only one person available to meet all your needs.

- **Relationality.** Meeting more connection needs with integrity.

- **Sexuality.** Nonmonogamy allows for further exploration of queerness and kink, more fun and adventure, and accommodation of desire discrepancies.

- **Growth and Expansion.** Broadening one's sense of self and creating a deeper connection and intimacy.

- **Pragmatism.** A practical way to live life and meet goals.

These are reasons that will help you craft meaning for your characters' relationships, settings, and sex.

Myth-Busting CNM

Dr. Zhana Vrangalova (n.d.), a leading sex educator and researcher on CNM, identifies information to bust myths about CNM in her course called Open Smarter. The following info consists of my takeaways from her class.

Myth 1: Monogamy Is the Ideal Relationship Style for Everyone

Monogamy to nonmonogamy is a spectrum or continuum. Some people will thrive with monogamy, others not. Many fail at all sorts of different points in monogamy, which speaks to individual natures, wants, and desire.

Myth 2: Nontraditional Relationship Styles Are for "Weird" People

As can happen with culture, family, or institutions, you may have been placed in a one-size-fits-all relationship box. But there are many people around you in different relationship constructions, with diverse wants, needs and sexual desires. How you consciously choose to weave this diversity into your character development will go a long way toward normalizing sexual differences.

Myth 3: There Must Be Zero Jealousy for Open Relationships to Work

Jealousy is a human emotion. It doesn't matter what type of relationship you choose to be in; you must learn to take information from jealousy and use it constructively. A disservice occurs when someone limits their choice of relationship type because they believe they will be jealous.

Conclusion

To appreciate this relational aspect of CNM, you may need to throw out old scripts, learn new information, and honor the choices that others make in the name of supporting them being their normal. As a writer, you have the opportunity to embrace all these things as you bring in factual information about relationship growth in Self and in characters. You have the ability to examine a relationship style that fits for your characters and bring it forward in a fictionally realistic and factually accurate state. Taking into account how the Self is presented through differentiation leaves you much to work with for your character's sexual development.

Bonus Activity

If you want to see different relationship dynamics in action, watch the Netflix series *How to Build a Sex Room*.

This series allows you to see sexual diversity and individual wants and desires. As you watch the construction of the ten rooms, note where you would place them on the sexual continuum. Every room created highlights different components of the individuals, couples, and groups. Consider how you would address those components if you were writing the world of the characters with their individual wants and needs. Be aware of the context; the show embodies everything sex-positive and nonjudgmental.

Session 9   Personalities to Help You Build Characters and Their Sex

When writing stories, many authors use personality tests to help build their characters. I've seen lots of workshops created to help you, the writer, figure out the inner workings of your characters. I have a different test to add to the mix. Like other research-based strategies in this book, it is based in science and brain chemistry. Interestingly enough, if you go through this process for yourself, you'll receive clarifying and experiential information about you, which will help you maintain separation from your characters. And you may find the answer to the age-old question, is it "opposites attract" or "birds of feather stick together?"

Introduction

The concept of love and its connection to personality has been extensively explored by Dr. Helen Fisher, a senior research fellow at The Kinsey Institute. Her work focuses on the biological and psychological underpinnings of human relationships, particularly romantic love.

In teaching human sexuality at the college level, students always wanted to discuss romance and relationships. I used Helen Fisher's Personality Model when I taught. On the first day of class, students took a battery of tests which I used for teaching concepts throughout the course. Fisher's application was by far a student favorite. Whenever we did group projects, I would assembly the students together based on these structures. I tied it to the idea of who would work well together.

When we held the class where I taught specifically about Fisher's personality model in regard to relationships, they had experienced it for half the semester. Most were floored with the results and many couldn't believe how right the tests were. They began to give family and friends the test. I took it with my partner. Most folks would not be surprised to find I fell into the Negotiator category and my love, the Director category as our primary expression of personality traits. Each of us as our secondary trait registered as Explorers. This will make more sense as an example as you read on.

Key Facts that drove Fisher's Research.

There are some basic research facts that were the underpinning of Fisher's research.

Background of Love

Psychologists have historically noted that people tend to fall in love with those from similar ethnic and socioeconomic backgrounds, intelligence levels, education, physical attractiveness, and shared values, such as religious, political, and social beliefs (Fisher 2016, 30).

Factors Influencing love

Love is influenced by proximity, timing, mutual affection, and the fulfillment of certain needs (Fisher 2016, 29).

Love Maps

People develop "Love Maps," which are lists of characteristics they desire in a partner, shaped by biology and experience (Fisher 2016, 26.)

Temperament, Genetics and Personality

Fisher summarizes personality as a combination of Temperament (biology) and Character (experiences). Traits like curiosity, creativity, novelty-seeking, compassion, cautiousness, and competitiveness are partly inherited. About 50% of personality variations are believed to be genetically linked (Fisher 2016, 30).

When Helen Fisher investigated the academic research and found that only four brain systems were linked to personality traits (Fisher 2016, 31), she focused her study to that information.

Dr. Fisher's Contributions

Fisher's research focus aimed to understand why people fall in love with certain individuals. Her investigation focused on how the personality types and biological temperaments influence romantic choices.

She created the Fisher Temperament Inventory FTI, a unique personality test based on brain architecture and physiology, different from other tests in its comprehensive approach to personality. The FTI's validity was confirmed using Functional Magnetic Resonance Imaging (fMRI) brain scanning, proving it accurately measures specific brain systems.

By focusing on the role of brain chemicals dopamine, serotonin, testosterone, and estrogen, in personality traits, she identified four primary personality types based on these brain systems: **Explorers (Dopamine), Builders (Serotonin), Directors (Testosterone),** and **Negotiators (Estrogen).** Each personality type tends to be drawn to certain types, with Explorers pairing with Explorers, Builders with Builders, and Directors often pairing with Negotiators, and vice versa.

The basic traits of each personality type as follows:

Explorers: Adventurous, spontaneous, risk-taking, and impulsive.

Builders: Calm, social, cautious, and orderly.

Directors: Direct, decisive, analytical, and independent.

Negotiators: Imaginative, intuitive, empathetic, and expressive.

Fisher deems the romantic attraction as a universal trait.

"…in a recent brain scanning study, both heterosexual and homosexual men and women lay in the scanner while they looked at photos of their beloveds. Those of both sexual orientations showed activity in the same basic brain pathways associated with feeling of intense romantic love Fisher 2016, 35)."

The chart of personality types I created will give you details and so will reading Fisher's work in depth.

Personality Type	Explorers-*Dopamine*	Builders-*Serotonin*	Directors-*Testosterone*	Negotiators-*Estrogen*
Romantic Preferences	Novelty-Seeking, Spontaneous, Energetic, Optimistic, Curious, Creative	Prefer Stable, Rule-Following Partners (Builder-Builder)	Attracted To Empathetic, Expressive Individuals (Director-Negotiator)	Drawn To Decisive, Logical Partners (Negotiator-Director)
Positive Traits	Playmate Novelty-Seeking, Spontaneous, Energetic, Optimistic, Curious, Creative	Helpmate Calm, Social, Cautious, Orderly, Persistent, Loyal, Traditional	Mindmate Direct, Decisive, Analytical, Logical, Independent, Strategic	Soulmate Imaginative, Intuitive, Empathetic, Expressive, Holistic, Idealistic
Negative Traits	Impulsive, Reckless, Unpredictable, Risk-Prone	Inflexible, Resistant To Change, Judgmental	Aloof, Insensitive, Blunt, Overly Pragmatic	Indecisive, Evasive, Overly Emotional, Scatterbrained
Descriptive Words	**Adventure**, Spontaneity, Energy, Fun, Traveling, Outgoing, Passion, Active	**Family**, Honesty, Moral, Respect, Loyal, Trust, Loving, Trustworthy	**Intelligent**, Intellectual, Debate, Ambition, Driven, Politics, Challenge, Real	**Passion**, Heart, Kindness, Sensitive, Reading, Sweet, Learning, Empathy
Self-Descriptor Words	Adventurous, Energetic, Impulsive, Curious, Novel	Calm, Social, Conscientious, Orderly, Traditional	Analytical, Decisive, Independent, Logical, Strategic	Imaginative, Intuitive, Empathetic, Expressive, Holistic

Potential Jobs	Travel Blogger, Adventure Guide, Entrepreneur, Artist, Photographer, Stock Trader	Teacher, Accountant, Lawyer, Civil Servant, Doctor, Librarian, Engineer	Ceo, Scientist, Engineer, Military Officer, Lawyer, Computer Programmer	Counselor, Therapist, Human Resources Manager, Diplomat, Teacher, Writer, Social Worker
Intimacy Questions	What Do You Do?	Who Do You Know?	What Projects Are In The Works?	How Do You Feel?
Other	Devoted to Experiences And Trust Impulses.	Feel Obligated to Larger Community, Trust Values.	Dedicated To Their Work. Skeptical. Seek Achievement and Trust Logic.	Devoted to Family, People, And Ideas. Trusting. Seek Harmony.

Application to Character Development in Writing

Fisher's research provides valuable insights for writers in crafting characters, enabling them to use personality types to define character traits, behaviors, and romantic dynamics. By understanding these personality dynamics, writers can create more nuanced and realistic characters and relationships.

Here are examples for each personality type:

Alex The Explorer (Dopamine):

Alex is an adventurous travel blogger who thrives on new experiences. He's spontaneous, often deciding on a whim to explore a new country. His social media is full of photos from his latest escapades, whether it's bungee jumping in New Zealand or backpacking through the Amazon. Alex is optimistic and energetic, always looking for the next thrill. However, his impulsiveness sometimes leads to reckless decisions, like when he spontaneously invested in a risky startup that failed.

Negative Aspects: Alex's constant need for novelty means he struggles with long-term commitments and often finds himself in financial difficulty due to his impulsive spending.

Emily A Builder (Serotonin):

Emily is a dedicated elementary school teacher who values stability and order. She loves routines and is highly organized, both in her professional and personal life. Emily is a pillar in her community, often volunteering for local events. She prefers quiet evenings at home or gatherings with close friends and family. Emily's cautious nature makes her a reliable and trustworthy friend.

Negative Aspects: Sometimes, Emily's need for control and predictability can make her inflexible and resistant to change. She can be judgmental of lifestyles that differ from her own conservative views.

Raj The Director (Testosterone):

Raj is an innovative tech entrepreneur known for his direct communication style and analytical thinking. He's highly focused on his work, often spending long hours at his startup. Raj is competitive and enjoys challenges, constantly seeking ways to improve his business. He's not very expressive emotionally but is deeply committed to his goals.

Negative Aspects: Raj's single-minded focus on work can make him seem aloof and uncaring in his personal relationships. He struggles with empathy and is often perceived as blunt or insensitive.

Sarah The Negotiator (Estrogen):

Sarah is a therapist known for her empathetic nature and strong interpersonal skills. She excels in understanding her clients' emotions and helping them articulate their feelings. Sarah is intuitive and often thinks holistically, considering various aspects of a problem. She's deeply involved in community service and advocates for mental health awareness.

Negative Aspects; Sarah's sensitivity sometimes leads her to take on too much emotional baggage from others. She can be indecisive and may avoid confrontations, which sometimes causes issues in her personal life.

Each personality type, as defined by Fisher, has its unique strengths and challenges, influencing how individuals interact with the world and form relationships. Understanding these types can be particularly useful in character development for storytelling, providing a framework for creating diverse and realistic personalities.

When pairing the similar or complementary personality types, certain dynamics can be observed, including reasons for compatibility and potential relational challenges.

Explorer with Explorer (Dopamine-Dopamine):

Compatibility: Two Explorers share a thirst for adventure and novelty. This pairing enjoys a relationship filled with spontaneity, excitement, and a mutual understanding of each other's need for personal freedom and exploration. They're likely to be very social, engaging in new activities together, and keeping the relationship dynamic and interesting.

Relational Challenges: The primary challenge for two Explorers is their shared impulsiveness and risk-taking, which might lead to instability in the relationship. Their focus on the present can result in a lack of long-term planning, financial instability, or difficulty in committing to long-term goals. Also, if their interests diverge, they might find themselves drifting apart due to a lack of shared direction.

Builder with Builder (Serotonin-Serotonin):

Compatibility: Builders value stability, tradition, and order, making two Builders highly compatible. This pair will likely appreciate a structured life, enjoying routines and shared values. They are likely to prioritize family and community, creating a stable and secure environment. Their mutual understanding of each other's need for predictability and order makes for a harmonious relationship.

Relational Challenges: The main issue for two Builders is their potential resistance to change and risk aversion. They might struggle in situations requiring adaptability or when faced with unexpected changes. This rigidity can also lead to a lack of spontaneity and excitement in the relationship. Additionally, their conformity to traditional values may cause issues if one partner starts questioning or deviating from these norms.

Director with Negotiator (Testosterone-Estrogen):

Compatibility: Directors and Negotiators often complement each other well. The Director's decisiveness and analytical mind pair nicely with the Negotiator's empathy and holistic thinking. Negotiators can provide emotional depth and understanding to the relationship, which can be grounding for the more reserved Directors. Directors, in turn, can provide structure and clarity, helping Negotiators focus their often broad-ranging interests.

Relational Challenges: The challenges in this pairing stem from their differing communication styles and emotional expressions. Directors may find Negotiators overly emotional or indecisive, while Negotiators might perceive Directors as emotionally detached or overly pragmatic. Negotiators' need for emotional connection and intimacy might clash with the Director's need for independence and space.

In each pairing, understanding and respecting each other's inherent personality traits are key to maintaining a balanced and fulfilling relationship. The challenges each pairing faces can often be mitigated through open communication, mutual respect, and a willingness to adapt to each other's needs.

Crafting Nuanced and Realistic Relationship Stories

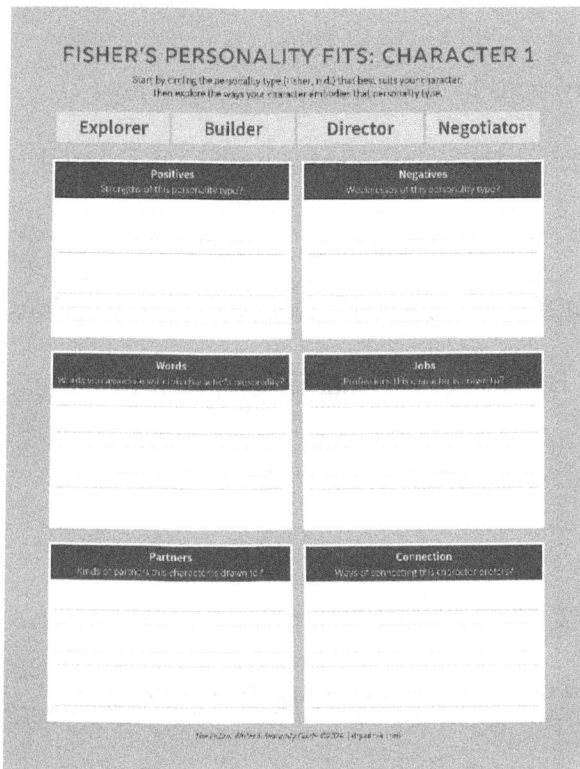

Fisher's work on personality types offers a wealth of insights that a writer can utilize to craft more nuanced and realistic relationship stories. Here's how a writer can apply her concepts to enhance their storytelling:

Character Development

Defining Characters: Use Fisher's personality types (Explorers, Builders, Directors, Negotiators) to create distinct, multidimensional characters. Each type has unique traits, motivations, and ways of interacting with the world, which can help in developing consistent and believable characters.

Depth and Complexity: Incorporate both the positive traits and the challenges associated with each personality type. This adds depth to characters and makes them more relatable and human.

Relationship Dynamics

Compatibility and Conflict: Understanding how different personality types interact can help in plotting out the dynamics of a relationship. For instance, a story about an Explorer and a Builder will naturally have tensions between the desire for novelty and stability, creating a rich ground for conflict and growth.

Character Growth: Characters can learn and grow from their relational experiences. For example, a Director learning to be more emotionally expressive due to their relationship with a Negotiator.

Plot Development

Driving the Narrative: Use the characters' personality traits to drive the story forward. For example, an Explorer's impulsive decision can set off a series of events that become the central plot of the story.

Creating Subplots: The interaction between different personality types can lead to various subplots, such as a secondary romance between two Builders or a friendship between an Explorer and a Director.

Conflict Resolution

Internal and External Conflicts: Fisher's model can be used to create both internal conflicts (e.g., a Builder struggling with their desire for change) and external conflicts (e.g., relationship challenges between a Negotiator and a Director).

Realistic Resolutions: Understanding these personality types can help in crafting realistic and satisfying resolutions to conflicts, as characters learn to navigate their differences and find common ground.

Dialogue and Interaction

Authentic Dialogue: Different personality types would communicate differently. An Explorer might use adventurous and energetic language, while a Builder might focus on stability and tradition. This can be reflected in their dialogue.

Interpersonal Dynamics: Knowing how different types interact can guide how characters would realistically behave in various situations, enhancing the authenticity of social interactions in the story.

Themes and Messages

Exploring Themes: Use the interaction between different personality types to explore themes like the importance of self-awareness, the value of compromise, and the beauty of embracing differences.

Conveying Messages: The story can convey messages about relationships, such as how understanding and respecting each other's individuality is key to a successful partnership.

Sexuality: You now have another framework with which to integrate character sexuality. Use Fisher's work to view the character and their sexuality and how they make choices. Think about who leads and who follows. Who is more like to have risky sexual behavior? What would the sexual behavior look like for each personality type based on their sex history. You have more information.

By using Fisher's framework, a writer can create a rich tapestry of characters and relationships that resonate with readers. Her research offers insights into human behavior and the complexities of love and relationships. When you place sexuality at the core, it becomes more illuminating.

You can take the test to see what it is like and deep dive into Helen Fisher's work to make it real ("Helen Fisher, PhD," n.d.) ("The Anatomy of Love," n.d.).

Brain science is powerful. You are seeing how it can help you craft a story, or understand personalities and additionally with details and specifics, how the chemicals work in sex. In the next chapter, keep the personalities types in mind as you watch the characters. And now you know the answer to the question about opposites attract and birds of a feather.

THE WRITING ELEMENTS FOR SEXUALITY

Session 10 Science: Storytelling. Play. Sex.

What type of brain chemistry do storytelling, play, and sex have in common?

When I think about storytelling, play, and sex, I think about a journey. Storytelling has a journey. Play has a journey. Sex has a journey. Each journey depends on all the things you have been addressing in this book so far. Each event has a goal. That goal depends on the protagonist. There will be obstacles and things that go wrong, but your protagonist deserves to reach their goal, yes? That is, whatever their goal is in the story journey or the sexual journey.

If the brain, which is considered the largest sex organ, is so important to sex, it's important to ask: How does the brain work in storytelling, and how are the brain and sex related?

This session starts with story—not one I will tell, but one that Paul Zak will tell.

Example 1: "Empathy, Neurochemistry, and the Dramatic Arc"

Go watch this five-minute video: "Empathy, Neurochemistry, and the Dramatic Arc" by Paul Zak (2013): https://www.youtube.com/watch?v=DHeqQAKHh3M#action=share.

As you watch, you can complete the worksheet provided to track your thinking.

Dissecting Zak's Work

As a writer, understanding these brain chemicals helps you craft your story in a way that keeps the reader involved. Zak showed the brain produced dopamine and oxytocin during the story. You start by introducing something new or surprising. Then, you build tension with challenges the characters must face, often because of past failures or crises. This leads to a climax where the characters have to confront their inner struggles to overcome the crisis. After this transformation, the story comes to a resolution.

Research into the effects of cortisol, dopamine, and oxytocin, particularly in storytelling and narrative engagement, is supported by various studies in the fields of neuroscience, psychology, and biology (Brockington et al. 2021).

Here's an overview:

Cortisol. In response to stress, the brain releases cortisol, which plays a crucial role in focusing attention and memory formation. Studies in neuroendocrinology have showed that cortisol, often released in response to perceived threats or stressful situations, can enhance memory consolidation of emotionally significant experiences. This concept is relevant in storytelling, as narratives that introduce tension or stress can increase listeners' or readers' attentiveness and memory retention. (Burke 2023)

Dopamine. The brain's reward system is connected to dopamine. It releases in response to pleasurable experiences and is associated with emotion, motivation, and engagement. Neuroscientific research has shown that engaging stories can stimulate the release of dopamine, which can enhance the audience's emotional response and keep them engaged with the narrative. This process is a key factor in why stories with emotionally charged content are often more captivating and memorable.

Science: Storytelling. Play. Sex.

Oxytocin. Oxytocin plays a known role in social bonding, empathy, and trust. Research in psychology and neuroscience has suggested emotional storytelling, particularly stories that involve interpersonal relationships and emotional connections, can stimulate that oxytocin release.

This hormone's role in empathy and social bonding may explain why narratives that foster a sense of connection and empathy are powerful in maintaining audience engagement and fostering a deeper emotional response. (Humm 2023)

As an author, knowing some brain chemistry helps you focus on how to tell your story to keep the reader in it. When you create tension, stress, and even peril in your story, readers become attentive because of cortisol. When you provide emotion in the story, it taps into engagement with dopamine. And when character narratives deeply connect with the reader, it triggers the release of oxytocin, which maintains reader engagement.

SCIENCE OF STORYTELLING
Questions on "The Magical Science of Storytelling" by David JP Phillips (2017)

What is the significance of the eBay story?

What is the significance of the Bond story?

What core element caused people to buy something in both stories?

What does Phillips use the story about falling in love to show?

What is the "angel's cocktail"?

What is the "devil's cocktail"?

Example 2: "The Magical Science of Storytelling"

Here is your second video, fifteen minutes: "The Magical Science of Storytelling" by David JP Phillips: https://www.youtube.com/watch?v=Nj-hdQMa3uA. Use the questions on the companion worksheet to guide your thinking.

Applying Phillips's Work

I loved Phillips's "functional storytelling" components:

1. Everyone is a storyteller from birth. Believe it.

2. Write your stories.

3. Index those stories for what they do. Which ones are the "make people laugh" with endorphins stories? Which stories make people feel empathy?

When you know your stories and which hormone they release and where, you can get the result you want from your readers and/or listeners.

The Brain on Story: *Wired for Story*

In her book, *Wired for Story*, Lisa Cron (2012) (Creative, Penn, 2021) addresses the brain chemistry of writing processes. Here are highlights from the twelve headings of her book:

Hook

"How to hook the reader: We think in story, which allows us to envision the future…the reader must want to know what happens next" (7). That's your writing job.

Focus

"How to zero in on your point: When the brain focuses its full attention on something, it filters out all unnecessary information" (24). Only give information when it's needed. You, the author, know everything—and you can dole it out in a fashion that adds to the engagement, because you will know the sex history and backstory of all your characters.

Emotion

"I'll feel what he's feeling: Emotion determines the meaning of everything." Think of it like pressing a button. As a writer, you are installing emotion buttons throughout the story. When the reader gets to the emotion, your writing will activate the button for them. Cron says, "All story is emotion based. If we're not feeling, we're not reading" (45). When producing a movie or writing a book, give readers the details in such a way that they can relate. When you do, the parts of their brains that would physically experience the events respond as if the readers are physically living the story. The more emotion there is, the stronger the reaction is in the person. That is why the meaning of sex is so important. The way the body moves reflects the emotional meaning.

Goal

"What does your protagonist really want? Everything we do is goal directed, and our biggest goal is figuring out everyone else's agenda, the better to achieve our own" (66). Without a clear goal, where is the protagonist going? Help your reader develop a sense of empathy with the main character so the reader cares what's happening with them. If your reader can't cheer for the protagonist, then they're just not going to get pulled into the story. Think back to the story about walking in the zoo from Paul Zak's video. Make his idea relate to the sexuality goals.

Worldview

"Digging up your protagonist's inner issue: We see the world not as it is, but as we believe it to be." Cron explains that, as the writer, you need to know when and why the protagonist's worldview was misaligned (85). This is true not only for the story overall, but for the protagonist's sexual history.

Specifics

"The story is in the specifics: We don't think in abstract; we think in specific images" (104). Give us the specifics, because, as Cron adds, "anything conceptual, abstract, or general must be made tangible in the protagonist's specific struggle" (104). Information must not be given as a stand-alone component, but woven into other things to make the connections. I did this for you by having you watch two videos to make the abstract concepts real as part of your journey through this book.

Also, use strong words and trim the details.

As a writer, your job is to prioritize for the reader. You've got to pick out the several bits that are truly important to the story and cut out the rest. Be careful with the details you give. If you give them, use them. Your reader's brain wants to make sense of them, not be frustrated by them if they don't have a purpose.

Also, avoid the cliché, overused, and passive words. When you use specific words in your description, they cause your reader's brain to light up. Chantilly lace, raspberry tea, bamboo wind chimes. Your brain goes to the exact experience, and you can have it with the characters in your story.

Conflict

"Courting conflict, the agent of change: The brain is wired to stubbornly resist change, even good change." Cron says that providing "unavoidable conflict" is the agent of change (125). You have to have conflict in the story to hold someone's attention.

Cause and Effect

"Cause and effect: From birth, our brain's primary goal is to make causal connections—if this, then that" (145). Your story must follow this path. Active voice lights up in the brain; passive voice doesn't. Read: "Someone was hitting the ball" vs. "He hit the ball." Your brain anticipates what is going to happen next. The more you give specific details in the active voice, the more the reader or listener will experience the sensations and feelings.

Science: Storytelling. Play. Sex.

Lessons

"What can go wrong, must go wrong—and then some: The brain uses stories to stimulate how we might navigate difficult situations in the future" (167). As the author, you can test the protagonist and give the reader much more: a satisfying story and a potential future lesson.

Patterns

"The road from setup to payoff: Since the brain abhors randomness, it's always converting raw data into meaningful patterns, the better to anticipate what might happen next." Cron elaborates, "To your reader, everything is either a setup, a payoff or the road in between" (186). Sex is a perfect medium for this type of writing, especially if you have hidden pieces of sex history that you can draw from.

The Past

"Meanwhile, back at the ranch: The brain summons past memories to evaluate what's happening in the moment in order to make sense of it." Cron explains that the techniques of foreshadowing, flashbacks, and subplots must help to create that order for the reader by providing information related to the main storyline (201). This is a great way to think of the sex thread in the weaving analogy.

New Pathways

"The writer's brain on story: It takes long-term, conscious effort to hone a skill before the brain assigns it to the cognitive unconscious." Because of this, Cron states, "There's no writing; there's only rewriting" (220). The act of learning new information and applying it over and over creates new pathways of understanding. This is the case with sexuality.

If you consider that the brain responds to how you put a story together, you have a new way to conceptualize your work. The same is true for understanding those chemicals regarding sex.

Also, think about stories within a story. Can you share the sex dialogue, backstory, and internalization in story form? Create little circles of stories within the big story. Loop ideas back to beginning points for better understanding.

Create a Play Practice in Sex (and Writing)

The following section about play is adapted from an article I published through Rosy Wellness in [2022] called "Create a Play Practice in Sex—Your Brain Will Thank You."

State of play stimulates the brain chemistry hormones, just like in storytelling. ("Play and the Feel Good Hormones," n.d.) (Robinson, n.d.)

Your play practice begins early in life. As a baby, you came into the world playing. You moved your arms and legs, sucked on your fingers, and found delight in the new world. That marks the beginning of a lifetime of play-discovery in movement and connection.

Play allows you to learn.

There are several play-practice areas where you grow, beginning at birth. You can learn as you discover your body (unoccupied play), play alone (solitary play), watch others play (spectator/onlooker behavior), play beside another (parallel play), play in an area of another and interact (associate play), and at last, play together out of an interest in the activity (cooperative play).

As you play, your brain develops the skills of cooperation, imagination, and risk-taking. The good news is you don't have to leave this learning behind. In fact, you can continue your

Science: Storytelling. Play. Sex.

brain growth in adult play. While you can find many places in your life to play, there is a specific adult-play activity, structured or unstructured—sex.

Your Brain on Play

Dr. Stuart Brown (2008) lays out a taxonomy for adult play in his TED Talk, "Play is More Than Just Fun." He begins his discussion with play signals. It's easy to first show this concept through your pets.

Think of a dog getting your attention to play. You see a dropped ball, toy, or stick at your feet. Then the downward dog bow follows with an enthusiastic tail wag. It's universal. You know they have signaled play.

But humans have a state of play, too. You have signals. Vocal. Facial. Body. Gestural. What do you picture or hear? Think about the people in your life. How do you know they have entered play mode? What are the obvious cues? How do you share that sexual play interest? This clarity is important to consider because when you use your play signals, you build safety and trust.

When playing, you go into an altered state with complex brain processes. Humans are unique and designed to play over a lifetime. Play is for survival. When you don't play, your brain shrinks.

Maybe my favorite part of Dr. Brown's video is when he suggests you look at your play history. Go back as far as you can in your memory to the most clear, joyful image you have. The point is to extract the emotion from that wonderful image, whether it is an event, birthday, vacation, or object, and carry that emotion forward in time. Bringing emotions forward keeps them alive in your actions today and allows them to expand.

You can integrate play into your everyday life, and when you do that, you are seeking balance. If you do this with sexuality, you'll have a more empowered sex life.

As a writer, if you take on a perspective of sex as play, you will have a new element, or strand of your weaving thread, to work with for your characters. When you think of sex play as a part of the holistic character, again, you have more to work with. How the character learned about play and engaged in it is part of the character history. It is now an element that is tied to the *why* of behavior and we can extrapolate into sexuality. Hopefully, you see play and sex as another example that sexuality does not occur in a vacuum. It is a unique and individualist part of the character as they have grown. You are diving deep to explore their sexuality foundations for their use and enjoyment in your story.

Types of Play for Fun's Sake

You can easily find many types of childhood play that mirror the process and structure of play "in the bedroom." (Note that "bedroom" doesn't mean the bedroom is the only location. Choose your spot or your character's spot based on the type of adult play and the location that fits best for you/your character. Fit your play to the perfect space.)

Ritual play. This involves games with rules and structure. Characters could be watching or playing. Create, strategize, and design activities that bring your characters together for a common purpose or goal. Think of consent for play, BDSM, or adding other people to their sexy time. The elements of rules and structure apply to setting up boundaries, providing agency, and allow for clarity within sexual relationships.

Rough and tumble. When your characters are physical with another person, you must identify their feelings and emotions for the sake of regulation; your characters may need to share them for safety and intimacy. Maybe your characters are rolling around tickling each other in a tickle war. Or you might up the excitement level with a chasing game for a kiss or hug.

Imagination. Explore. What if? Here you can use fantasy that might include reading erotica or role-playing.

Body play. Think of the spontaneous desire to get ourselves out of gravity. Perhaps your character is nude, jumping up and down on the bed with a partner. Perhaps a pillow fight ensues. How does their body feel? How does the partner's body look?

Object play. Manipulation of objects, building, and designing all fall into the object play category. This might be where you introduce body painting, drawing on the body with markers, sex toys. Think of props.

Beneficial Side Effects of Play Practice

If you need more specific reasons for play, science backs it by showing that play improves cognitive functioning, reduces stress, unlocks that creative thinking, creates experiences of childlike exuberance, and results in just plain laughing more often, which releases feel-good chemicals in your body.

So, if you haven't considered sex as play practice, now is your chance. Elevate your curiosity and see what others have done. Unlock your imagination and create something new.

Story affects your brain, and play affects your brain through the state of play stimulating brain chemistry hormones ("Play and the Feel Good Hormones," n.d.). By adding active words rather than passive word, as outlined in Lisa Cron's cause-and-effect highlights (Cron 2012, 145) while your character's activities produce chemical movement in your readers brain, you will provide the reader with a full sensory experience.

The Brain on Sex: The Chemicals

I hope you see know why I put the brain work together, on story, on sex, and on play. The wonderful brain chemistry is active in all three areas. Now let's look at sex and brain chemicals.

The brain's control over sexual behavior is primarily through hormones and neurotransmitters. Deshmukh et al. n.d.)(2) **Testosterone**, crucial for both men and women, is essential for sexual arousal and orgasm. Its low levels can dampen excitement and orgasmic response. **Estrogen** also plays a significant role in regulating sexual behaviors in both sexes.

Neurotransmitters, which are chemical messengers, play a pivotal role in sexual desire, arousal, orgasm, and partner preference. These include oxytocin, serotonin, dopamine, and vasopressin. Following orgasm, increased levels of serotonin, oxytocin, and vasopressin contribute to feelings of pleasure, motivation, relaxation, reduced pain sensitivity, and foster intimacy and attachment.

Vasopressin is associated with aggression, memory, and concentration. Hormonal changes trigger a biological desire for sex, with testosterone being the primary driver in men. In women, the limbic system (associated with memory, fear, and aggression) is initially activated. Since sex releases dopamine, the 'pleasure chemical,' it becomes a sought-after sensory experience. This dopamine release also occurs with other enjoyable activities like eating, learning, or listening to music, as the brain processes these pleasures similarly.

During sexual activity, a rise in **nitric oxide** leads to physical responses like flushing and erect nipples and sends blood flow into the erectile areas in the penis and clitoris. ("Biology of Female Sexual Function» Sexual Medicine» BUMC" n.d.) (Biga et al. 2019)

Dopamine and **epinephrine** levels increase with sexual stimulation, enhancing enjoyment. (McKinney, n.d.)

At the **orgasmic climax**, the hypothalamus activates, releasing oxytocin and increasing dopamine levels. This process leads to physical responses like vaginal contractions. Oxytocin counters cortisol, a major stress hormone, and fosters a sense of trust and longing for the partner. However, high levels of testosterone might inhibit the activity of oxytocin, affecting this connection.

Post-orgasm, **serotonin** is released, often leading to drowsiness and a desire to rest.

When you understand the body responses chemically during sexual arousal and activity, you can write with clarity. This is from understanding the specific body responses, and then adding the emotions for those responses.

Sex Journey as a Dramatic Arc

Sexual activity, as a story component, has a beginning, middle, and end. You can apply all the elements addressed by Zak, Phillips, Cron, Brown, Schnarch, and Fisher to write the sex in individual scenes, or to make the sexual journey into the primary story.

As writers, when we understand that storytelling, play, and sex all activate brain chemicals, we can now see more clearly that sex itself is a storytelling component. When we write it, with intent and understanding of brain function and chemicals, we control the journey of the reader in the brain. And now we have a trifecta of chemical activity to use in writing.

In some ways, you may get a bigger bang when using sex in scene because some of the same chemicals emerge when reading about sex as when having sex. Think of creating a special character cocktail, like Phillips discussed, but now layering in even more ingredients. If you understand how the brain works on sex, how the brain works on story, and how the brain works on play, you've mastered more than most who write sex.

As you focus on the meaning of sexual activity (as discussed in Session 7), you'll have more connections to your character with which to work. Your writing will more clearly weave in sex, the characters' context and experience, and the why from the characters' sexual histories.

Session 11 A Scene with Sex

How Do You Write a Scene with Sex?

This chapter brings us to the actual scene-with-sex writing. This is the reason you thought you came here for—how do you write a scene with sex? In this new paradigm, you've actually been writing scenes with sex all along as you addressed bits and pieces to let us experience the sexuality of the character. So, this scene with sex is one that is up close and physically personal. But with the material you've learned so far, I hope you see that you have so much to work with to create your scene with sex. You can use a holistic frame from which to pull your content to make the scene rock and roll. You have emotion and motivation. If you look back at character development, including sex history and play history; your setting; your events; and your information to be revealed in the scene, you now will see a scene structure to apply.

The Idea of Scene Types: Break Your Scene Down

You have arrived at the place to put the scene types discussed in Session 7 into action. Go through these elements and answer the questions about where your scene is going.

- **Number.** How many characters will be in your scene? One character, two characters, a small group, a large group, or a crowd?

- **Surroundings.** Indoors or outdoors?

- **Action.** What is occurring in the scene? Is there an unexpected element in this scene?

- **Tension.** How will the tension of this scene push characters to "choice points" (Watts et al. n.d.)? The character arrives at a point in the scene and has to make choices to move the story forward. These choices will become clearer in the section below on the 5 Cs of Scene.

- **Variety.** Have you used this location for a scene before?

You can use these elements of scene construction to either create the scene or revise and tighten what you've already written.

I have also found it helpful to harken back to asking the basic questions about each scene: who, what, when, why, where, and how?

Now let's move to what I call the spine of the scene: the **5 Cs of Scene**.

Editor Heather Whitaker's Grand Unified Theory of Writing

Life gives you so many wonderful things. I never imagined the first editor I met and worked with would have a science background in physics, much less that she would apply that to understanding writing and story structure. This took my love of systems theory to a new place. I consider Heather Whitaker's ideas of writing to be elegant.

Like in physics, she believes there are basic laws that govern writing.

In writing, these laws apply to everything from the overall plot down to the dialogue within a scene to the punctuation in a sentence.

Have you noticed that chapters vary in length?

Paragraphs vary in length?

Sentences vary in length?

Did you realize that you use the same technique to change them up—quicker pace, slower pace?

Have you noticed there are the wants and needs of the character in the overall story, and also specific wants and needs in individual scenes? If you've written a scene well, the wants and needs in the scene connect to the overarching wants and needs in the story. And if you understand the importance of that connection, then you can apply it to how you pull all the information that you need into the scene.

What occurs at the story level also occurs at a scene level. You can use the same tools to build the scene that you would use to support the overall story evolution.

Think of it this way: *A good scene is like a novel in miniature.*

"To really make a scene pop, you need to complete a compressed story and character arc, like a miniaturized version of an entire novel's arc," says Heather Whitaker (pers. comm. July 7, 2022). All elements in the story are applied at scene level and story level.

Furthermore, in creating your scene with sex, you will pull threads from all the information addressed in previous sessions of this book. They include:

1. The holistic nature of the character

2. PEMS and sex positivity

3. PLISSIT

4. Eliminating author intrusion while being clear about what you, the author, bring to the story

5. Brain science of storytelling, play, and sex

6. The character's sex history, personality, and differentiation of self

7. MICE—pulling drivers of milieu, idea, character, and event together for conflict, tension and emotion

8. Your overall story arc, and how it applies to the specific arc within your scene

Let's refer back to your macro lens and micro lens (the big picture and the closer picture). Now that we are focusing only on the scene level, I want to introduce you to the idea of the **mezzo lens**. If the micro lens now addresses the paragraphs and the words that make up one

SEXUALITY AT THE SCENE LEVEL

Describe how the following sexuality concepts will apply to the specific scene you're constructing.

The Holistic Nature of the Character	PEMS and Sex Positivity
PLISSIT	Eliminating Author Intrusion While Being Informed by Author Emotions
Brain Science of Storytelling, Play, and Sex	Character's Sex History, Personality, and Differentiation of Self
MICE	Macro, Micro, Mezzo: How Does Your Overall Story Arc Inform This Scene?

scene, the mezzo lens addresses the overall arc of that scene, and the macro lens addresses the overall arc of the story informing the scene.

Consider the scenes as building blocks of the full story. In the same way, your paragraphs are the building blocks of the scene, so when you've strung together all the paragraphs to make the scenes, all the scenes create your overarching story.

Heather Whitaker's 5 Cs of Scene

In two classes I took with Heather Whitaker (September 2017; January 2019), each one year long, the Grand Unified Theory of Writing was presented on a story level and on a scene level. The following information comprises my takeaways from her courses.

You can stop at each scene and determine where it fits in telling your story—building your story—as well as each paragraph to determine where it fits in the scene. The five elements are: catalyst, complications, crisis, climax, and consequences. You may have specific attachments to these words that make it difficult to understand the structure, so I've added other words I think also describe the five elements the story and scene must have.

Catalyst

The **catalyst** may be your hook. It's the thing that changes the character's normal life. It is the event or revelation at the start of the story or scene that creates a new problem. So, when you talk about the structure of the story, you want to identify specifically the event or the information at the start of the story that creates the journey (or at the mezzo level, the problem the character is going to address). The information that comes before the event is introduced should describe how you see the character in their natural world. When the new element is added, you can then show how it changes the character's world and how they move forward because of it.

Alternate words for catalyst include motivation, stimulus, initiating event, or inciting event.

Complications

In a race to save someone, what actions, words, or revelations occur to add to the tension? **Complications** are actions, dialogue, or revelations that add to mounting conflict or tension, internal and external. They are information revealed. The emotion of the information mounts to a sense of conflict that leaves your reader with a thought like, "Whoa, this is getting really intense."

By raising the intensity level, you are setting a stage for your reader to feel that when a decision is made, it is going to be important. This is where obstacles are thrown in the way of the character. You see the path toward a goal intensify with the notion of working hard to get to it.

Perhaps someone is racing to save that baby in a stroller rolling into the path of an oncoming car of a distracted driver. The domino effect begins. What things are put in the path of the character that affect the character's journey and their determination to save the baby? How do they fit with the character getting what they want? A bicyclist crosses in front of the hero. The character's shoe flies off. They hop forward, continuing after the stroller, and trip over an open manhole cover. You get the point. Complications are the things thrown in the way of the hero to stop them from reaching their goal. They are the same types of things you will take from the character's sex history and tailor into obstacles blocking the goals related to sex in both story and scene.

Alternate words for complications include difficulties, conflicts, or obstacles.

Crisis

The **crisis** is the moment that the protagonist identifies the specific choices available to them. I like to think about it as character growth through differentiation of the Self in the midst of a dilemma. Their options are revealed as they run, hide, or stand up for themselves. This is the *clarity of the dilemma.* When writing this part, also ask how it is being laid out: Is it a two-choice dilemma? A three-choice dilemma?

Alternate words for crisis include dilemma, choice, option, or possibility.

Climax

The **climax** is the point in the scene or story where the character actively makes the decision. It is the *decisive moment.* Decision made. Consent given. With the decision made, the actions in the scene or story unfold based on that decision, and you experience how those actions affect the rest of the scene or story.

Alternate words for climax include decisive moment, decision, choice, or course of action selected.

Consequences

The consequences occur when the actions of the decision are complete. This is how you create resolution. This is where you show how the decision and subsequent actions affect the story.

Perhaps it is *discovery*. A decision was made, actions were taken, new information emerged, and consequences from actions resulted.

Alternate words for consequences include results, outcomes, effects, upshots, reactions, or resolutions.

The 5 Cs in Scenes with Sex

The 5 Cs of Scene are important elements to note. They represent the backbone, or the spine, of the scene and the story. And when you look at it that way, you can make bullet outlines and identify each of these things in the story and scenes. For now, you'll want to determine if you can find all the parts when analyzing a scene that's already written out. These five elements make the scene complete. And remember, you can always address them in revisions.

So, if writing is constructed for character change, these 5 Cs of Scene elements may make it clear why it's important to write a scene with sex as you go, rather than skip it to write later. Yes, this is an element overlooked by writers where sex is concerned. Even if you write the scene poorly (in your estimation), you will still have an idea of the growth that was made by the character when you go forward into the rest of the story you're telling. I suggest you work to put the scene in without writing "insert sex here."

Using these elements is also an easy way to take a look at scene structure. Pick scene favorites, of yours or from other writers, and identify the elements. If you pick a scene with sex, you'll be able to look for the 5 Cs; determine if they are wrapped in the emotion, narrative, and setting; and find the places that move you forward in the story. This exercise is a way for you to recognize why certain writing resonates with you. You can pull that learning into the way you think about how your characters respond in your story and scenes.

Activity 1: Model Analysis of Scene from "Buns of Steel"

I've included a link to a series of four scenes that build on one another to tell a story. Below the link, I analyze the first episode, "Buns of Steel."

Link: https://qr1.be/X9TE

Let's start with outlining the basics:

- Who: Les, Sol, and Conrad introduced

- What: Mutual sex/love interest

- When: Sunday morning

- Where: The motorcycle garage shop

- Why: Sol gets the ball rolling—tired of waiting

- How: He invites Les to the garage

The 5 Cs of Les's POV

- **Catalyst (what causes change).** "Sol stood next to his bike, with his back to me, naked."

- **Complications (what adds tension and conflict).** "Maybe you need to check the clock over the desk." Les has arrived in Sol's private time. Sol turns, and Les sees the whole package she always wanted.

- **Crisis (clarity of choice).** First, "No, just the opposite. He told me he'd love to have me as part of the family and he knew how you felt. I didn't believe him." Then, "What? I'd had it wrong all this time. I'd been holding back. Not anymore." Then, "It's a test." And finally, "I had to know [Sol's thinking]."

- **Climax (decision made and action taken).** First, "Maybe you'll believe me." Then, "I stepped forward." Finally, "Kiss me, Sol."

- **Consequences (resolution of the scene with new info).** "Now go put on your coveralls 'cause those buns of steel with their accompanying parts are mine. And I have a test for you, too."

For now, I've used this scene to look at just the structural elements, but we'll use other stories for discussion of the language, emotion of sex writing, and characters' sex movement, including an annotated story at the end of the book.

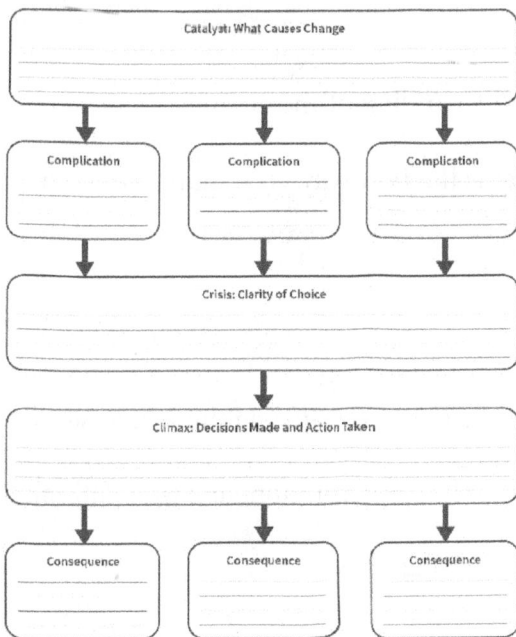

THE 5 CS OF SCENE

Create a scene or select a written scene and identify the components of Heather Whitaker's 5 Cs.

Catalyst: What Causes Change

Complication

Complication

Complication

Crisis: Clarity of Choice

Climax: Decisions Made and Action Taken

Consequence

Consequence

Consequence

The Fiction Writer's Sexuality Guide ©2024 | RC Rauth-or.com

Activity 2: Identify the 5 Cs of a Chosen Scene

It's your turn.

You can choose a scene of your own or a favorite scene. This is all about practice. The more you can find the 5 Cs, the easier it will be to use them for story or scene creation and for self-editing. Use the template on the companion worksheet to organize your analysis.

Activity 3: Evaluate a Scene with Sex

Choose a scene with sex, one you've written or one you love, and mark the 5 Cs.

With the same template, begin to add in the wants, needs, and/or motivation parts. My first published story was edited with this template. I held my breath as Heather read it, marking these points after I had filled in the meanings. I wanted to show that my erotic story was built upon a solid writing foundation. And it was.

Further Evaluation

You can also begin to assess your chosen scene with these questions.

- What does the scene accomplish?

- What is revealed about the character?

- Whose POV?

- How does this scene deepen the reader's understanding of the character?

- What needs to be revealed? To whom? What is the best way? (Often the best way is what is most vulnerable—human connection.)

Analyzing Your Own Scenes

The scene needs to hang on the desire, want, or need of the character, during the whole story and the individual moments of the scene. Action is wrapped in history, emotion, and motivation. Name those components so you know what you are showcasing.

If you've built characters with different experiences, then there are automatic conflicts, internal and external, with which to work. Show them.

I lay the printed pages out in a row and find the Cs visually. If the first C happens on the third page of five, maybe you have too much exposition. If the fourth and fifth Cs happen on the same page as each other, maybe more information is needed for context in the scene. Think of mapping your arc visually with these five points.

These five elements also let you get an early look at the pace and timing of the scene. Remember that the type of sex and the things you want to reveal about the character can be varied. What tension are you building with emotion? What is the meaning of the characters' connection here? Are you at the beginning, middle, or end of that connection? How might each stage look different?

Sex itself has an arc. Notice I didn't say romance. Even if characters meet and immediately have a sexual encounter, that's the starting point for the sexual arc. What will happen next, and how will it end? Sex is a journey longer than moments of orgasm. Maybe orgasm isn't a climactic component for your character. The way the characters do sex could be based on traditional gender roles, or a different script. All of that is embodied in the sex created in the scene, but the scenes are created from the holistic nature of the characters.

Remember, sex is a huge element of human nature. Sex is for self-development. It is a huge part of our personal/character growth. The height of intimacy is showing something about yourself to a partner before you know it yourself; that is vulnerability. The partner becomes a witness to your growth. That awareness will shine through in the scenes you create.

A Scene with Sex

Ask different questions like in the next checklist to get your scene in place for your story.

SCENE CONSTRUCTION CHECKLIST

Use this checklist to help you navigate the parts of your scene—or scenes you read from other authors. You may discover areas you want to refine. Use this information to help you create a bank of examples; they will help you learn and grow in your writing.

Opening

- [ ] Was I pulled into the POV character's situation immediately?

Character

- [ ] Did I get a sense of their identity?
- [ ] Did I get a sense of their wants and needs?
- [ ] Could I "see" them to some degree?
- [ ] Did their emotion come through?

Plot

- [ ] Did I understand what was happening?
- [ ] Were characters working toward individual goals?
- [ ] Did the storyline keep me interested?

Setting

- [ ] Did I feel like a part of the scene?
- [ ] Details? (Enough, too little, too much?)

Dialogue

- [ ] Did I know who was speaking?
- [ ] Enough dialogue? (Or too little, too much?)

Pacing

- [ ] Did the scene flow well? (Or too slow, too fast?)
- [ ] Was I able to follow the events as they happened?

Description

- [ ] Could I see what was happening clearly?
- [ ] Strong imagery used?
- [ ] Did I skim, or feel distracted as I read?
- [ ] Was it interesting?
- [ ] Was more detail needed to make the scene feel more important or real?

Voice

- [ ] Was the writing unique in some way?
- [ ] Did I feel like only this writer could write this story?
- [ ] Did the viewpoint feel authentic?

Ending

- [ ] Did it feel complete?
- [ ] Did the scene end on a cliffhanger or create the urge to read on?

Session 12 The Language and Emotional Beats of Sex Writing

How Do You Describe Body Parts?

At the end of the day, remember John Grisham's fear of describing body parts. As authors, you choose your words to suit your stories and your characters. You use them to create tension, describe sensations and settings, and create interesting dialogue. But how do you learn to use the language of sex?

I hope that question moved you right into your Person-of-the-Writer place. Did you ask yourself, what do I use? How did I come to use those words? Can I say those words aloud or in public to my family, my friends, or my lovers?

Sometimes people get so intent on writing about sex that they go overboard, thinking they have to describe everything that happens sexually, even if it's not accurate. Sometimes, they go in the opposite direction: The words are so technical. Trying to get them right, the author pulled you from the page and into an education lecture. Remember to only layer in the needed information.

I read many scenes with sex where I can tell what stumped the author. It may be the words, the lack of emotional intent, or the meaning of sex to the character. (It's not enough that they are horny. That's the symptom; go deeper.) It may be the real disconnect to the sex. Perhaps the scene with sex is there only because someone thought it should be, because sex sells. Or the author wrote the scene as a separate event, and not an event connected to the overall wants and needs of the character. Maybe nothing about the sex moved the story forward. Sex is an extension of a person and therefore a character. Use the character's sexual activity to understand them and help them grow.

In this chapter, you will hear about words and emotional beats. Consider this your word-bank chapter, which you can use as needed for your specific characters and continue to add to.

Education of the Body

How do you label body parts? What do you call body parts, or even the language of sex? What category would you classify the words as? Are they medical, scientific, accurate, colloquial, slang, dirty talk, or baby talk? Is the language specific to a region, culture, or group? There is more detail and nuance to consider. This is the depth of sexuality.

Many writers are only concerned with how to describe body parts and how to describe them functioning. Think back to John Grisham. That is how he framed it. I hope you will hold that idea in your head so you can be a writer who stops, considers, researches, and feels good about what they come up with for their characters, their meaning of sex, and their way of embodying emotion.

Keep in mind, the culture you live in likely uses a heteronormative frame for everything, including the couples and the actions in sex. Within that frame, PinV intercourse is expected to be the main course of sex. But does it have to be? If you are looking at sex as a journey and not a destination, you can ask how sex is constructed between characters. You get to be creative. Even if you normally write heterosexual characters, you might actually create characters that will resonate with queer people; you can maybe even fashion types of characters that allow people of other sexualities to feel represented in your stories. I'm asking you to step away from heteronormativity and let sexuality be the continuum it is. You can construct your characters to be whole characters actively living the sexuality in their body.

As an example, let's talk about the vulva and vagina. The vulva and the vagina are different parts of the body. The vulva is the external female genitalia. It is what a cisgender woman sees when she looks between her legs. The vagina is the internal female genitalia, or the canal inside the body that leads to the cervix. These two terms distinguish two different areas and are probably the most commonly misused. As an example, I've seen many writers talk about a "shaved vagina." Pubic hair that you can see or shave off is located externally, on the vulva up to the pubic bone.

Education of the Mind

Once you evaluate and assess how sexuality is presented in writing and in discussions, you will see the inequality and judgments everywhere. It is pervasive in all we do, and it takes steps, like learning to think and write about sex differently, to help change things.

Let me give you this example. In the genre of romance, you will see phrases that keep us stuck in an old paradigm about sex.

Do you write steamy or clean romance?

The implication of this word choice may imply that sex is dirty. "Clean" and "wholesome" romance may connote moral well-being. I've heard that closed-door romance writing, romance writing without explicit sex is now considered "sweet" romance to avoid that very implication. Since I promote sex with personal integrity, "clean" romance is a hard sell. But these are the kinds of questions to ask and think about when you are writing and talking. What are you promoting directly or indirectly, knowingly or unknowingly? Are you doing what's always been done?

As a writer, it is always better to be clear about what is going on in all aspects of your story. You are the captain of the ship.

Words are just words until you give them context to tell your story, but they're a good place to start. Let's take a look at potential word banks for different sexual labels and activities.

Words Related to Body Parts

Vulva-Owners

between their legs, box, bud, canal, their center, clitoris, clit, their core, crease, crevice, cunt, their entrance, their essence, femininity, flower, folds, groin, the heart of them, honeypot, inner lips, juncture of their thighs, labia, mons, mound, mouth of their arousal, nub, orifice, pink pearl, pool of moisture, pussy, quim, their sex, sheath, slit, vagina, vulva, womb

Penis-Owners

appendage, arousal, balls, bulge, cock, dick, erection, groin, their length, lingam, manhood, member, organ, package, penis, phallus, rod, sack, scrotum, their sex, shaft, stalk, stall, testicles

Words Related to PinV Intercourse

action between the sheets, bang, bed, bone, fuck, have sex, horizontal bop, lay with, make love, shag, take

Words Related to Positioning

anchor, bear (down on), bob, cover, encircle, grind, guide, lift, nestle, plump up, pin, raise, rest (between or against), rock (against), rotate, settle over (mouth or body), spread, straddle, surround, tangle/entangle, twine/entwine

Words Related to Penetration of Various Orifices

breach, burrow, bury, dart, delve, dip (into), embed, enter, fill, impale, insert, penetrate, pierce, plunge, press (down on or into), prick, probe, prod, push, ravage, settle (between or into), sheathe, shove, sink (into), spear, stab, stick, thrust, tunnel

Words for Genital Body Responses

Vulva-Owners

creamy, damp, drenched, flooded, glazed, glistening, juicy, moist, moisture, pooled, saturated, shimmering, slippery, succulent, swimming, thick, wet

Penis-Owners

alert, aroused, bulging, came to attention, chiseled, distended, erect, extended, flaunting, hard, jutting, large, plump, rigid, rosy, slushed, stiff, straining, swelling, taut, tense, tight, uptight

Sensual Language

What is sensual language? Sensual means "pertaining to, inclined to, or preoccupied with the gratification of the senses or appetites." Language is "a body of words and the systems for their use" (*Dictionary.com* n.d.). So, by combining those words, we can surmise that **sensual language** is a body of words used to describe the gratification of the senses. Here's a word bank to start. What will you add?

- ablaze, abrade, ache, aching, adventurous, afterglow, alive, aloft, ambience, animal, anxious, arch, arouse, artistic, attain, automated, awaken, awash
- beg, blaze, blush, boneless, breathless/breathlessly, bright, brush, bud of nerves/bundle of nerves
- calloused fingers, captivate, captivating, captive, caressed, caresses, catch, circle,

clasp, clench, clutch, core, cradle, creep, crescendo, crescent, crush, cry/cry out, cup, curl, curves, curvy

- delectable, delicious, delight, depths, devour, dilated, dizzy, drain, dreamy, dripping

- ecstasy, enflame, erotic, ethereal, euphoric, explosive, exquisite

- fathoms, feather-light, feathered, feathery, fierce, filled up, fire, firm, flamed, folds, fresh

- gently, glide, glittered, groaned, growl

- heat, heated, heavenly, heavy, helpless, home, honey, hot, hungered, husky

- ice, icy

- jolt

- kiss

- laced, languid, let go, lick, light, linger, liquid, luscious, lush, lust

- mesmerizing, mind-bending, moan, moist, moisture, molten, mound

- need, nibble, nip

- ooze, organic, orgasm

- panting, passion, peak, pearl of nerves, pebbled, pet, pinch, plump, plush, pressed, pressure, pulse, pulsing, pump, purr

- rapid, reach, relax, release, responsive, ripe, rosy, rub

- sated, satiny, scorched, scratch, scream, seductive, sensitive, sexy, sharp, sheath, shimmer, shiver, shivering, silent, sinful, sinking, sip, sizzling, skittered, slick, slid, slide, slipped, slippery, snared, soft, softly, sparked, squeeze, stars, stoke, strain, striking, stroke, strong, succulent, suck, suckle, sultry, sumptuous, surrender, sweet ache, swollen

- taste, tease, thick, tingle, throb, thrummed, thrust

- undulate

- velvet, vibrate

- warm, wet, whole, wicked

- yes

- zing, zip

Words to Suggest the Type of Touch

abrade, across, arouse, brand, brush, catch, clasp, cling, close (on or around), clutch, devote time to, drag, explore, feather, feel, finger, flex, flick, follow (the curve, line, or angle of), give, glide, grab, graze, grip, grope, handle, hold, inch, inflame, knead, linger, love, make love to, map, massage, move, nudge, nuzzle, outline, peel, pinch, plant (a kiss or hand), play, pleasure, possess, pull, ravish, roll (between), rub, run (along), savor, scale, scorch, scrape, sear, seduce, seize, skim, slide, slither, soothe, stretch, stroke, surge, sweep, swipe, swirl, take, tantalize, tap, tease, test, tickle, torture, trace, trail, trail (down, across, or up), treat to, tug, tweak, twist, weigh, wiggle, work, worship, wrap (arms, hands, self, around), wriggle, yank

Words for General Physical Appearance

attractive, breathtaking, chiseled, delectable, heavy, muscular, pale, perfection, rounded, sexy, shapely, solid, strong, tanned, thick, voluptuous

Words Describing Character Mannerisms and Sound

amorous, begging, blazing, blistering, bold, brazen, callous, charged, concentrating, contented, dainty, daring, desperate, dreamy, erotic, exposed, feverish, fiery, fragile, grasping, groaning, heated, innocent, intense, intimate, inviting, irresistible, lascivious, limp, lustful, moaning, muted, passionate, pointed, possessive, powerful, practiced, purring, reckless, roughened, satisfied, savage, seamy, shallow, sharp, spicy, steamy, sweet, tender, tousled, triumphant, vibrant, vulnerable, weak, welcoming, wicked

Words for How a Character Touches

aggressive, butterfly-soft, caressing, cleverly, deliberately, delicately, demanding, fast, feasting, feathered, firmly, furiously, gentle, gossamer, greedy, hovering, insistent, intertwined, light, lingering, needy, probing, rapid, rolling, roughly, savoring, settling, slow, soft, teasing, unsteady, urgent, wandering

Words for How Something Feels When Touched

accommodating, cool, delicious, firm, grasping, hot, pliant, scorching, shaking, silky, smooth, soft, supple, tender, warm, welcoming

Words for How a Character Moves in Reaction

adhering, bolting, clinging, erupting, jerking, parting, pulsating, quivering, shivering, shuddering, splaying, spreading, stirring, surging, swaying, thrashing, trembling, tremor

Words for What a Character Feels in Reaction

aching, anticipation, asking, awareness, bliss, building, burn, craving, crested, divine, drunk, echoing, electric, enchanting, entrancing, euphoric, exciting, exhilarating, exquisite, fire, flaming, flooding, full, havoc, heavenly, humming, indescribable, intoxicating, knot, magical, melting, overloading, overpowering, peaking, pulsing, quicken, radiating, rush, searing, sensitive, shock, simmering, singing, sparking, spike, stirring, stunned, thrilling, throbbing, thumping, thundering, tingling, vibrating, warm, weightless, yearning

Your Words

You can add to your word bank here as your characters change. No one uses the exact same language. You may get creative. Remember, characters may make up their own words for their own reasons. Here is a resource, called *The Language of Lust, Love, Sex*, that you might find helpful: https://www.sex-lexis.com.

Final Note on Words

Sometimes it helps to break your thinking down into these types of categories. You may add other ways to conceptualize this to your toolbox. Just consider your use of sensual language. Continue adding to your bank of words. As you write your micro tension, consider using cadence and rhythm to represent breath in the characters' spoken language as a way of mounting the tension: "Yes. Yes. Yes."

Writing the Emotional Beats

Let's switch gears to the emotions of sex. If characters are exchanging emotions, how do you write that? According to Katherine Cowley (2014), you use emotional story beats and dialogue. **Emotional beats** occur when the action in the story or scene causes an emotional response in the character. Those emotions become the fuel that will support the character in making their next move. We want to be clear about them in relation to sex.

The macro level of emotional beats is the overall character motivation in the story. The micro level is the character motivation in the specific scene. Both types of motivation are based in emotion, and that is what we see wrapped around sex.

Cowley (2014) considers these four types of description to be the basic emotional beats:

1. Internal Physical Sensations

2. External Physical Sensations

3. Physical Action

4. State the Emotion ("Key 7")

She says a fifth emotional beat is:

5. Use something distinctive to your character or story world ("Key 8")

She considers the last five to be advanced emotional beats, which should be used

sparingly for variation:

6. Setting

7. Metaphor or Simile

8. Mini Flashback

9. Mini Flashforward

10. Surreal Imagery ("Key 9")

Examples of Emotional Beats

In the spirit of Cowley's method of demonstrating these emotional beats, I took one line of

dialogue and crafted it into ten different emotional beats.

I use two characters, and have Amie speaking to Rick. Rick will be the POV character, so

he will be the one having the emotions in these examples. Imagine the depth of material you will

have if you know the characters' wants and needs. This activity can help you get clear on what

you know as well as how the emotional beats might help you.

If you practice these components, you'll get in the habit of using them in your writing.

You could write every one of these beats in a particular place in your story where you want the punch, and then decide which one best serves the characters and the scene. You choose what fits in your space.

Meet Amie and Rick. As you read each set, note what you feel and what you learn about the character.

Internal Physical Sensations

The first type of emotional beat describes an internal physical sensation, like so:

> "So, it doesn't bother you I've bedded other people," said Amie.

> Butterflies danced in Rick's stomach. He detested being the leader in sex.

External Physical Sensations

The second beat describes an external sensation:

> "So, it doesn't bother you I've bedded other people," said Amie.

> A sunbeam passed over Rick's face. He looked up and smiled at the warmth.

Physical Actions

The third beat uses physical actions:

> "So, it doesn't bother you I've bedded other people," said Amie.

> Rick blew out a breath as his shoulders dropped. *Yes.* That's one less worry for tonight's events.

State the Emotion

The fourth beat involves stating the emotion in the narration:

> "So, it doesn't bother you I've bedded other people," said Amie.

> Relief spread through Rick. He liked equal partnering and looked forward to what she would bring to their sexual picnic.

Detail Particular to Character or Story World

The fifth beat is accomplished by describing something from the specific world of your characters:

> "So, it doesn't bother you I've bedded other people," said Amie.
>
> Only a sex educator could deliver her sexual history information in such a sexy, inviting manner.

Setting

The sixth beat involves the character noticing something significant from their surroundings:

> "So, it doesn't bother you I've bedded other people," said Amie.
>
> Rick's gaze shifted from Amie to her luxurious queen bed. The ghosts of the past lived there, and he believed they gave her confidence and positive energy.

Metaphor or Simile

The seventh beat brings in figurative language:

> "So, it doesn't bother you I've bedded other people," said Amie.
>
> Rick's eyes were drawn to her mouth. She grinned, and her lips glistened like dew on a rose.

Mini Flashback

The eighth beat uses a momentary flashback to convey emotion:

> "So, it doesn't bother you I've bedded other people," said Amie.
>
> The first time Rick had heard those words, they intimidated him. Today, he took them for what they were: information.

Mini Flashforward

The ninth beat uses a momentary flashforward:

"So, it doesn't bother you I've bedded other people," said Amie.

Tomorrow, if she offered him the opportunity to join her with some of those people, he'd

accept it.

Surreal Images

The tenth and final beat draws emotion from a surreal image:

"So, it doesn't bother you I've bedded other people," said Amie.

Amie's words excited Rick. The bed grew arms and motioned him forward.

Your Turn: Assessing the Written Beats

I hope the examples helped you see how you can deliver emotions in different ways. This is
about adding more tools to your toolbox. Use the companion worksheet to practice writing these
beats on your own.

PRACTICE THE SEXUAL EMOTIONAL BEATS

Choose a scene with sex that features two characters. Select a sentence of dialogue spoken by one,
then write the other's reaction in ten different ways, using a different emotional beat each time (Cowley 2014).

Starting Sentence

Emotional Beat Responses

1. Internal physical sensation:
2. External physical sensation:
3. Physical action:
4. State the emotion:
5. Use something distinctive to your character or story world:
6. Setting:
7. Metaphor or simile:
8. Mini flashback:
9. Mini flashforward:
10. Surreal imagery:

The Fiction Writer's Sensuality Guide ©2024 | drjadear.com

Reflection

You can ask the following questions to reflect
once you've practiced the beats on your own:

1.   Which beat was the easiest to write? Which
was the hardest? This may show you overuse of
one type of beat in your writing style.

2. Which beat brought forward information you found important and interesting?

3. What would happen if you changed the word "bedded" to fucked, copulated, screwed, or bonked? Your reader gathers information about the character in your world through the character's use and delivery of language. You might be foreshadowing, showing an element of fear, or revealing an aspect of the relationship dynamics.

4. Was one beat style more suited for your story, character, or setting? Remember variation is your friend.

Closeness and Connection

Let me pause and remind you of Jodie Archer and Matthew Jockers (2016). After data mining bestsellers, they created an algorithm based on what the books had in common. They learned that elements of human closeness and human connection are significant in bestsellers. Readers are drawn to shared chemistry, shared bonds, and people communicating in moments of shared intimacy. Readers want characters to experience moments of closeness.

Fifty Shades of Grey (James 2015) had come out as they started this venture. They wondered if sex made the book a bestseller. While there was a lot of sex in the book (new sex to some), when they compared it to other bestsellers, they learned that sex was the *tool* used to show connection and closeness. Their research identified that the story was about the intimacy of Christian and Ana and their character transformation.

You Can Become a Sex Writing Weaver

What does this session on words and emotional beats continue to help you do?

1. Get clear on your character's Self vs. your Self

2. Create your character's sex history timeline in the character bible and identify PEMS

3. Identify the 5 Cs structure to write a scene. Knowing where you are in your scene/story structure allows you to track the emotional components, so you place them where they are most effective in telling the story and having the reader join in the feeling.

4. Name *why* the character is having a sexual moment. Why sex now? Revelations, connection? Add character motivation for sex. Think vulnerability—how sex tells you *more*. Can your character meet their partner where they are? Stand up and show themself a part they've never seen before in front of another person?

5. Weave the physical in between dialogue. Think about the emotion and meaning. Which type of physical sex displays the emotion best? The type of sex reveals personality and depth of the characters.

I hope you see that your characters have a starting point for growth in your story on their own sexual continuum. You know where your characters are because of sex history and PEMS. Knowing this information helps you choose the right words and emotions. In writing, tools like sex are only as good as the user. How do you use your characters' sex? Let's go find out.

Session 13 The Movement of Sex: Solo, Between, and Among Characters

Introduction

Now you are armed with a perspective of sex positivity. Using sex in your writing with the clarity that emotion is key is a new paradigm. Here are some questions to consider as you move people's bodies in scenes with sex.

- What can bodies do?

- Which bodies are doing them?

- What movements fit the characters' development in your story?

First, my writer friends, keep your clothes on.

Second, give yourself permission to create body position activities. This is both mental and physical.

As a way for you, the Person of the Writer, to tap into emotions, you will get active here as you stage body movements.

Let's start with an individual character.

Solo Sexual Pleasure

Solo sex is a great way to show the empowerment of an individual, their interest in sex, and their well-being. Identify the type or level of interest on a continuum. Where is that movement going to begin? Consider that the starting point for character growth. Where will they end? Sex may be the perfect vehicle to show a character taking charge, stepping into something new, or owning who they are. Some questions and ideas:

- Exploration and discovery allow you to introduce sexual items and concepts.

- What would solo sex look like for the body type or gender type of your character?

- What would it be like to be in the character's skin, with their life obstacles, sex history, and relationship desires?

- List the emotions that might arise.

- What is the context of the solo sex? How will that bring the character forward in the story?

- What items do you have for solo sex? For example: lube, toys, condoms for covering insertable toys, clean-up solutions, arousal oils, CBD oils, and fetish items.

Determine where on the continuum of sex your character is at the start of the story. That may be anywhere from "I never masturbate" to "Masturbation is a regular component of my life and I love to experiment."

Direct the Scene with Solo Sex

First, select a solo sexual pleasure idea, and second, put yourself in the mindset of a director of a movie scene.

Next, identify your setting. Will the setting create obstacles? For example, did the heat go out an hour before the session was to begin? How can you use that for tension in the scene?

Then identify your pleasure tools. Are these familiar or unfamiliar to the character? How will they be introduced?

Consider having a conversation with your character about their wants and needs. You are the director. Name what the focus of the scene is. How many times have you heard actors say, "What is my motivation?" Give the character the right motivation.

Remember, if you were to watch a porn scene to get the physical ideas, there would be no meaning and emotion, no deep character wants and needs. That is a difference between porn and writing fiction. With the emotion, you can create depth through sex.

Direct the Scene with Partnered Sexual Pleasure

Again, keep your clothes on, and grab a willing partner to go through the movement mechanics. While the real focus is the emotion, your actual mechanics are important. You don't want your readers wondering if a person is physically safe or thinking about how the body doesn't bend a certain way and getting pulled out of the scene.

Consider what is easy, what is difficult, and what is doable. What is valuable about this activity is you will have *feelings* as you go through it. Document them. They will help you consider the added element of emotion that can come into play.

For example: What is it like to be nose-to-nose in a specific seated position on your partner? What is it like to have your butt up in the air and know your partner is seeing that part of you?

Those are two possibilities, but the important point is the POV of the character. How do they feel about the physical thing that is going on?

If you have layered it with their wants and needs, then the fears, excitement, and anxiety—whether internal or external—will come through. How will this scene assist the growth of the character? Empowerment? New discovery? Self-validation?

Look at the place in the scene where the character might process what is going on for them and that will help you write it well. Think of the scene as having a background and foreground, like in a picture. Get up close with the emotion in the foreground while the physical activity is in the background. See what that looks like, then switch it around: Get up close with the physical activity while the emotion is in the background, and see what that looks like.

What if your character is neurodivergent? What if they are physically disabled or have a mental health condition? What if they have an invisible disability? How would those traits change your character's approach to or invitation for sexual intimacy? How would they change the characters' sex positions? What is the scene like with characters who have the same body parts? Different body parts?

I hope by now you have moved away from an automatic PinV-intercourse way of thinking. As I said at the beginning of this book, most folks think PinV sex when they hear the phrase "sex scenes." But when you do use PinV sex, remember that there are only so many ways to have PinV sex. What makes your PinV sex interesting is the characters' individuality, their history, and their wants and needs. Remember to keep these ideas with the characters and use them in the motion of sex.

If you need coupled body specifics, go look at the pictures in the *Kama Sutra*. Take sex apart and put it back together. It does not have to be a straight line to PinV intercourse. Maybe that's not even on the menu. And remember, there are three orifices for penetration. Are your characters interested, not interested in using those spaces for sex? What do they like to do?

What keeps the scene from getting boring is the emotional content; I reiterate that the meaning of the sex determines the type of sex. You will write about physical sensations, but when you bring forward the physical, emotional, mental, *and* spiritual levels of sex, that is when you choose to be your most vulnerable.

For some, naked skin and intimate parts uncovered feel vulnerable. Some may be preoccupied with their body, performance, or skill levels. These are things that lack of sex education has caused us to focus on. You can use these preoccupations as an arc of change for your characters. Could they push past them and think differently about themselves at the end?

For others, being naked is nothing, and it is their emotions which make them vulnerable. When you use the sex history, which could include anything from bad sex, to yearning for something different, to a poor relationship, to no sexual debut yet, to bad familial role models— all of that sits in the middle of the scene. These are things that provide revealing moments through sex between your characters.

Preparation is key. When you know your character's sexual history and how they feel about sex and their body, and then have two people coming together for sexual activity, that knowledge gives you great tension. How can you project the consequences of how your participants feel, both about sex and about themselves, into the scene with sex? What would happen? What might elevate them individually in the scene? What obstacle would make them squirm? Using these elements, you connect to the characters, see why they might fit as a couple, and root for them to get all the pleasure they can from being with one another.

Direct the Scene with Group Sexual Pleasure

You will need to become your own continuity supervisor. Which feet, which hands, which breasts, which penises? Where are the clothes? I accidentally put away the lube that I didn't introduce into the scene. Yes, pesky details, just like life.

Sometimes people throw in the sex because they think sex sells. Instead, use sex to show character movement and growth. If the character is in a polyamorous or CNM relationship, these are things to use and consider in the scene. Where are tension points and why? When you consider that information, the physical activity will be easier to create. What are the roles, rules, and boundaries being set up? And again, why?

The Sexual Menu

To get clarity between ourselves and our characters, let's create individual sexual menus. Most of us understand that a "chef" cooking at home for themselves is a little different than them cooking for or with someone else. Try your hand at naming different options.

I like to use a menu to consider the possible activities. Put your character in a restaurant. What is the style of their restaurant? The type of restaurant? Vegan? Italian? This choice communicates something about the whole character. Translate this to sex. Celibate? Monogamous? Polyamorous? Consensually nonmonogamous?

What Is on Their Sexual Menu?

Is there something that is a limited offer only? Are there seasonal offerings? It's St. Patrick's Day—is there a special of the day? It's fall and the sweet potatoes are in—is the meal at the whim of the chef? Did the chef feel creative and put these items together? Examples of menu items could be fetish play, role play, BDSM, and vanilla sex.

Is this dinner for one? Dinner for two? Dinner for a group?

How Have They Created and Constructed the Menu?

Does the menu have a variety of options? Cocktails. Appetizers. Proteins. Main course. Sides. Desserts.

Does it have allure? How is it being presented?

Is What Is Offered Clearly Described?

Don't make the patrons of the restaurant do all the work to find what a character offers. Be clear. Upfront. Describe the sexual activity that is being offered in detail.

Imagine two restaurant chefs as they come together with different ideas about how things will be created, presented, and savored. Use these natural differences to grow your characters.

Can You Have It Your Way?

Negotiations.

For example: "I'd like the kale salad with the cranberries and pine nuts, and leave off the parmesan cheese. Also, I'm not a fan of the poppyseed dressing—could I have the vinaigrette instead? Oh, and I'm allergic to peanuts, so can you make sure those pine nuts haven't been near any?"

Do people have as much trouble asking for exactly what they want in food establishments as they do when it comes to sex? Maybe you can use that idea to extrapolate how to have that clarity in sexual negotiations.

Do You Connect with a Restaurant Ahead of Time?

If you need more information about a restaurant, you may clarify timing, space, weather, and types of food ahead of time. That's what you would do in preparation to make sure you get what you want. Could you think about that as a concept in the scene with sex?

Create A Sexual Menu

Make the sexual menu a DIY event. Get the paper and pens and imagine yourself as a sexy restaurant with offerings for patrons. What are your headings? What is the special? What makes it change? Let yourself get closer to your character's action by getting clear on your action. Then make one for the character—or you may find it easier to start with the character. Go with what fits for you.

Sexual Menu Du Jour
Special of the Day

Cocktails

Appetizers

Main Course

Sides

Dessert

The Fiction Writer's Sexuality Guide ©2024 | drjauthor.com

Phases of Sex

Let's consider writing about sex in two phases. The first phase is "outside the bedroom" (nonphysical to light physical sexual activity) and the second is "inside the bedroom intimate physical sexual activity." And for discussing these phases, consider the *bedroom* to be a figurative place. (It is wherever the sexual body parts are coming into contact. The characters are now close together, physically, emotionally, mentally, and spiritually.)

What are all the things that can go on before intimate physical activity happens? Did you put phone sex on the sexual menu? What if each character uses dirty talk or masturbates over the phone? Consider where the activity is in context of the arc of character growth. At the beginning of a connection, these activities will have a different emotional feel than when the characters share them further down the road in their character arc. Learn to stop and ask how the embodiment of the emotion at the moment best serves your reader seeing character growth.

In the "outside the bedroom" phase, your characters are still away from each other physically with sexual contact, but intimacy, connection, and vulnerability are happening. These are things on the sexual continuum; they *are* sexual. They just aren't up close and personal yet. But I would label a phone call where dirty talk and self-touching are happening as a scene with sex. You need to practice a new way to think about it.

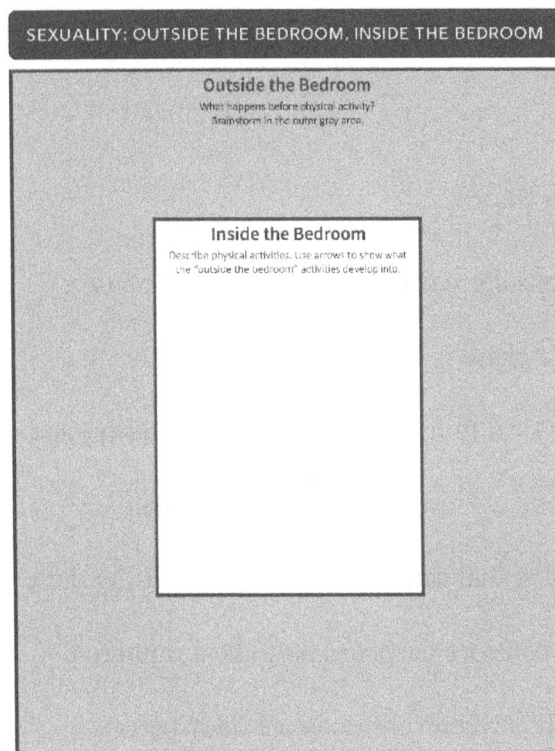

SEXUALITY: OUTSIDE THE BEDROOM, INSIDE THE BEDROOM

Outside the Bedroom

What happens before physical activity?
Brainstorm in the outer gray area.

Inside the Bedroom

Describe physical activities. Use arrows to show what
the "outside the bedroom" activities develop into.

The Demon Writer's Sexuality Guide © 2024 | djsauthor.com

In Conclusion

Body parts and their movements can get mixed, tied up, or just plain messy, but now you should have a plan to keep you grounded. If you have worked your weaving magic leading up to the scene and are asking various and systemic questions, writing about body parts will be easier.

The Final Session

One More Idea

You and I have pulled together a lot of content in these past sessions to write your stories and consider your scenes with sex. And yet, I have another idea for you to contemplate. I hope you place it in your toolbox to use for crafting your story.

There Is a Destination in Growth to Work Toward

For great sex in relation to your characters and their growth, it is helpful and necessary to know where you are headed with your story and character arcs, and to know where you are going with sex. This may not happen in the first draft, but you will be able to revise your work and make it shine in the next draft. The question is, will you know the end when you get there?

To answer that question, I want to refer you to one more set of strategies that works toward a sexually healthy adult.

With this behavioral composite, you have a way to measure where your character is in their growth and the areas or amounts of movement, you'd like for them to make through their story progression. You will also have tangible points to use as parts of character development. Now, let's add another dimension.

What Is Magnificent Sex: Reality or Aspiration?

What makes great sex?

Isn't that a part of what you want to show in your story and scene?

Magnificent Sex is a book based on the research of Peggy Kleinplatz and A. Dana Ménard (2020). They studied good sex, not bad sex. They categorized sex as good sex, very good sex, and great sex.

The researchers determined there are eight elements for magnificent sex:

1. Immerse yourself fully in the present moment, being physically present, concentrating fully, and deeply engaged (20).

2. When you're with someone else, it centers around forming a connection, aligning with each other, and achieving harmony. This is often referred to as a union (22).

3. Active listening by both partners fosters a foundation of mutual respect and trust, leading to profound sexual experiences and erotic closeness (25).

4. In terms of communication, it's essential to blend clear communication with profound empathy, discussing sex openly for mutual understanding. The exchange of physical and emotional intimacy can be dynamic, captivating, intense, clear, and welcoming. Using touch as a means of communication serves to refresh one's understanding of their partner and their body (26).

5. Your true self matters. Embrace being real, sincere, and open. Extraordinary sex involves seizing the chance to be wholly and truly yourself, as well as being unrestrained during the act. Experiencing such exceptional sex means allowing yourself to indulge in pleasure and fully savor the experience. It is in these moments of extraordinary intimacy that you truly discover who you are (27).

6. In the realm of extraordinary sexual experiences, the ideas of vulnerability and surrender become prominent. Individuals opt to expose their deepest emotions while being

completely visible to another (28). If you recall from Session 8, this is also a component of differentiation.

7. Extraordinary sex involves exploration, taking risks in relationships, enjoyment, playfulness, and challenging or broadening personal limits (30). Do you still engage in self-exploration, let alone in exploring your sexuality?

8. Extraordinary sex encompasses transcendent experiences, elevating mental, emotional, physical, spiritual, and relational aspects. It's a surreal experience that inherently fosters growth, affirms life, and brings transformative changes. Exceptional sex is nothing like the stereotypes portrayed in media. For the best sexual experiences, introspection is key. Often, the necessary risks required to achieve such high-quality sexual encounters are not fully considered (31).

It is important to note that all magnificent sex experiences comprised the same eight components (34).

Activity: Imagine

Let's revisit the sexual menu idea again, but this time considering it in recipe form.

A recipe is selected to taste, to fit a particular mood. Let's say you're making cookies, like in *Magnificent Sex*. You decide on chocolate chip cookies. Consider the basics of tailoring a recipe for the chocolate chip cookies. You could use chocolate, or perhaps something changes your mind, and you use butterscotch chips. You could use larger chunks than normal, or you could add nuts. Which type of nuts? You could spoon the cookies out differently for baking. You know the height or thickness of the cookies, and you know which length of time will make them crispy vs. soft and chewy.

Sex, like cookies, is about variation and tailoring to the moment. You can see potential for new and fun exploration when it's tied to what you want, whether it's cookies or sex.

For your characters, you can ask, how do intense pleasure and high levels of built-up arousal contribute to sexual encounters of magnificent sex? Maybe creating specific sexual recipes with a co-chef is how one attains their personal sexual growth.

Final Thoughts

In this guide, I hope you have taken the permission I've offered and used it for you, the Person and you, the Writer. I hope you give yourself the permission to explore your sexual ideas, thoughts, and feelings as the author.

You have permission to explore the sexuality of your characters.

Create customized templates to help you make that exploration.

Continue to explore the resources outlined in this book and those you collect to embellish the depth of your characters.

My goal has been to provide enough information for you to step into your strength about writing sex and write it rather than avoid it. I hope I helped you alter your thinking processes and gain a new perspective or lens to consider sex in your scenes and stories.

As always, use this content from my research and my life to get the characters rolling in your scenes with sex. Be the person who strives for extraordinary sexuality in life and writing. And remember, sex is a journey just like writing is a journey. The outcome can be orgasmic, but if you add up all the pleasure minutes together, there are more minutes in the journey than the outcome. Enjoy them all.

Writing Scenes with Sex: An Annotated Erotic Story

Have you ever wanted to sit beside someone and learn how they write sex? You can watch the process, but you won't necessarily understand the choices. What if you could see their processes during the edit, or the revision, with the reasons for what they are doing spelled out? Or, even better, a final product annotated with those processes for every single line? That's what this section is.

In a 4,000-word short story, which is now the beginning of a novella I am writing, I provide that. This annotated work serves as a full product highlighting the material in *A Fiction Writer's Guide to Sexuality: Sex—It's More Than a Scene.*

I documented elements addressed throughout the guide. From a clear definition of sexuality with all its components, to anchoring sex from the beginning of the story, to the meaning and motivation of the sexual activity itself—this annotation documents the holistic aspects of showcasing sexuality in your character for the entire piece of writing. Your sexuality is with you every day, every moment, whether you acknowledge it or not. It is no different for the characters.

As a writer, you research everything you can to create the best story for the best characters. My hope is that with this annotation, if you are scared to write sex, you will see that it is only one element that can be learned about and addressed. And while you learn, you will have a vehicle to assess and evaluate your own meanings and motivations for sex: you, the Person of the Writer. In doing it this way, you not only will learn about yourself, but you will have a clear starting point for the boundaries between you and your characters. You will know that the character's sex is not your sex.

I indicated this annotation is of a short story that is now the first chapter of a novella. This demonstrates a valuable point about the writing process. A story and a scene contain the same elements. There is the macro view (the overall story and narrative) and the micro view (the scene level). That means that each scene is a complete building block of a larger story. The story in the scene has an arc, the character's movement has an arc, and the sexuality sits proudly in the middle, ready to be used to highlight the characters' wants and needs for your scene within your story.

This is a clear example of writing holistically. When you hold onto the idea that your character is a sexual being, and you understand their narrative of sexual development (their sex history), you honor the whole person of the character. In turn, you honor your own sexuality. You have moved yourself from a writer who is simply writing a story to a writer who considers the world they live in and represents their characters with dignity—dignity through writing these full characters in what I call a factually accurate and fictionally realistic way. You teach, whether or not you signed up for it. Intention is a part of the author's journey. Sexuality gets added to the intention when you make an effort to be sex-positive.

This annotation offers a succinct template to access sexual content in a meaningful way to enrich the development of your characters.

Remember, in the annotation that follows, you are looking at a final story product that has gone through multiple rounds of revision. While I used the methods named in the annotation during my initial writing, I also utilized them in edits and revisions. Whether a pantser or a plotter, you can use this book, either in part or in whole, to solidify the sexuality of your characters.

What I have done in this annotation is exactly what I expected of myself as an educator, therapist, and supervisor. I explained the use of my sentences with theoretical reasons. This is essentially an application-based learning product. If you study the writing craft and can name the components behind my choices, then you can also look to see if you've incorporated them into your work.

Evaluating your characters' sexuality is no different than assessing passive vs. active voice, or looking to see if the characters are moving forward out of their wants and needs in the face of the obstacles you place in front of them. With all the information I've provided, I hope it will help you normalize sexuality and allow your characters to have it as a natural part of who they are.

Whether it was the actual physical scene with sex or the fear of judgment that kept you from writing, when you know why you are writing, you'll work with a confidence many authors don't have.

"Forever Tattooed," by Dr. J.

Am I a jerk, an S&M junkie, or a sucker for romance? [1] This ink shop may have turned me into all three. [2] Watching women pressured by group think come in here every day, choosing some meaningless shit to have inked on their bodies, exasperated me. [3] So, I let them feed my sadist nature while I teased them with the talk about the pain of tattooing and I laced it with sexual innuendo. [4] Abraham always snatched one away if he believed I had gone too far with my banter. Since he knew me so well, he'd send me to my office to beat it off. [5] Why couldn't they understand that adding a tattoo to their skin was like having a life event seared into their total persona? [6]

It was for me. It was for her. [7]

After Lorelei died at the hands of a texting bastard, I didn't think I could live. [8] If it weren't for my crew at Tattooed Forever, I would have drunk myself into a stupor and never come out of my house. [9] They pushed and prodded, reminding me that I had to live every day to honor her memory. [10]

Slowly, I got my act together and dragged myself back to the place where we had memorialized our love. [11] Two years after her death, I had yet to feel anything like the connection I'd had with Lorelei. That all changed the day *she* walked in the door. [12]

Weekends were busy at the shop and on this day, a group of sorority girls tied up our time. Each inker worked double-time. Afterward, the girls huddled around each other, admiring their fresh ink through the clear, plastic wrap bandages as the door opened, and she ambled in. [13] Standing in the middle of girl mayhem, this woman stole the show. [14] Yeah, she looked good with her long wavy hair and a curvy body, but there was more. She appeared like an accidental, exotic flower placed in a bouquet of ragged wildflowers. Something else radiated off

Annotations for "Forever Tattooed"

1. Character elements in the form of questions. Each element signifies a part of Gabe's personality. Sexuality thread anchored. Micro tension sits in the choices.

2. Setting identified for story and Gabe's personality.

3. "Meaningless" ink upsets Gabe. Foreshadowing.

4. Behaviors activate Gabe's sadistic nature, and Gabe lets it play out. Foreshadowing.

5. Ally-Abraham monitors Gabe going off the rails and took care of him the last time, but Gabe sits with the pain.

6. Symbolism. Meaning of tattoo to Gabe.

7. Gabe's history and connection between tattoos and Lorelei. Point in sex history.

8. Gabe consumed by grief.

9. Community support of him. Setting supports Gabe.

10. Friends help him refocus to positive aspect of Lorelei.

11. Layered meanings of setting: work; where they memorialized love; tattoo; love; sex.

12. **C1: CATALYST.** New problem. Time and emotional connection to today.

13. Tattoo shop setting. Typical environment occurring when heroine walks in.

14. Contrast of "woman" to college "girls."

her. She held a determination and sureness about her. Everyone else dropped away from my sight. Moving over to the counter, she exuded a confidence bound with grace and elegance. [15]

"I got this, Gabe." Abraham started toward her. His movement broke my trance, and I grabbed his arm. [16]

"No, I do." As Abraham turned, I held resolve in my eyes. His expression told me he was questioning my motives again, but he nodded and stepped aside. [17]

She opened the sample book on the counter and looked over our products. By the time I reached her side, she had the pages open to my pain. My tattoo pics stared back at me. [18]

Lorelei. I could smell her fragrance. [19]

The woman caressed the lips-kiss-tattoo on the pelvic bone that marked the gateway to arousal on Lorelei's body. We each had inked the same place. The tattoo was ours. The reason, the idea, the meaning behind why we had done it reminded me it had been real. As she continued touching the tattoo in the picture, I flashed back to Lorelei, laughing and smiling after our fuck for the ages. Miss Exotic Flower looked up and searched my face. Focused on the picture, I swallowed hard as I attempted to control the emotion surging in me. [20] Glancing back at the book, she smiled. I kicked my brain back into gear.

"Looking to get inked today?" [21]

As she turned and faced me, I got a close glimpse into a set of crystal-blue eyes that shimmered like deep water off an island pier. How could eyes so vibrant and cool make me so hot and unsettled? [22] Lorelei's scent grew stronger. My dick twitched, reminding me I was in a room full of people. [23]

15. Illustrating the aspects of Gabe's connections and response to the woman. Body elements and persona contrast. Total demeanor awakened Gabe and pulled him in.

16. **C2: COMPLICATION/OBSTACLE.** Abraham interrupts the moment.

17. Abraham's interactions suggest another cycle of concern regarding Gabe's destructive self-behavior.

18. **C2: COMPLICATION/OBSTACLE.** Gabe's tattoo pictures. Slow reveal begins.

19. **C2: COMPLICATION/OBSTACLE.** The past becomes the present.

20. Woman touches lip tattoo and unleashes bittersweet memories of Lorelei for Gabe.

21. Woman's smile moves Gabe back into the present. Action. Response. Differentiation.

22. PEMS response to eyes. Emotional beat. Metaphor.

23. **C2: COMPLICATION/OBSTACLE.** PEMS body response to olfactory memory of Lorelei. Physical by smell and body reaction through Emotion and Mental

"Maybe that, and a lot more." She delivered her words with a practiced precision while she scanned me over. [24] I heated up. The last time I felt this sensation had been before Lorelei died. [25]

"Gabe?"

"Yeah, do I know you?"

"No, but I'd know you anywhere by description." [26] She closed the binder, picked it up, and settled it to her chest before propping her chin on the edge of it. Her face softened with a faraway look and yet she maintained a distinct connection with me. "Is there someplace private where we can talk?" [27]

Her words hit me like the downstroke on a stuck bolt being loosened from old, unused machinery. Sexual desire that had begun as a trickle now rushed through me with the force of Niagara Falls. The idea of my body bending, twisting, and pounding her played like a porn movie in my head. [28] With that vision, I decided to show her to an ink room and not my office. In my private space, I would be all over her and I'd never hear the end of it from Abraham. [29]

"Let's go down the hall. First room on the right." Abraham threw me a quizzical look as I ushered her back. [30] She clutched the tattoo sample book to her chest until we got to the room. [31] When she sat, she placed it on her lap and stared at me. This sensation inside me felt eerily familiar. [32]

I cleared my throat. "Okay, talk." [33] Her demeanor had shifted in the time we'd walked from the front room to this room. I was at a loss as to what it was about. She was not your typical person looking for a tat. I mean, she could sport a tattoo, but she wasn't our clientele. [34] Her shining eyes kept sending out messages that my dick wanted to address, even though she hadn't yet used words to tell me what she wanted. [35]

24. Foreshadowing.

25. **C2: COMPLICATION/OBSTACLE.** PEMS sexual reaction marked by Lorelei.

26. Woman reveals a connection—that she knows him.

27. Use of setting and the binder; Gabe connected to woman. Foreshadowing.

28. PEMS sexual reaction to "someplace private." Emotional beat: metaphor.

29. Gabe regulates emotion (differentiation); brain kicks in.

30. Setting transition. More private, but with ally paying attention.

31. Woman clutches his memories close to the heart.

32. Woman gets what she wants. Action and response; a "this is it" moment. Gabe senses it.

33. Cutting off the feeling; Gabe addresses her. Differentiation.

34. Her behavior changes and Gabe struggles to make sense of it. Did he miss something? Is this jerk behavior? Refer back to original questions in the first paragraph.

35. Gabe notes his sexual response to her.

"Well, you are brusque. I thought I could do this, but I can't. I thought it would be easier. Who am I kidding? This would never be easy." [36] She lifted her nice ass off the chair, but I moved in front of her and she settled back down. [37]

"Most people get a little nervous about the prospect of being inked. It's normal. Look, there's no equipment out, so this is a friendly consultation." [38]

The forced laugh that emanated from her throat sounded sexy. *Is she having a sexual reaction, like me?* [39]

Setting the book aside, she opened her purse and withdrew an envelope. She sighed and handed me the worn and tattered paper. [40] Her arm shook like a bridge in a storm. [41] I reached out to take the paper. It resonated with my skin, and something about it sent a message to my DNA, fiery and familiar. [42]

The address line read Dana Parker. [43] My mind was slow on the uptake and my heart neared an explosion as the handwriting and return address registered in my brain. *Lorelei.* I staggered a step back and caught the doorjamb in my side. [44]

Focusing on the woman in front of me, I calmed my breathing. "This is you. You're Dana?" She nodded yes. "This is from Lorelei." [45]

"The letter explains everything. Just read it." [46]

"Read it? You waltz in here and cause my blood to rise and then give me a jolt from the past." [47]

"I know you don't know me, but I know you. Wait, did you say I caused your blood to rise?" She peeked at my crotch. [48]

"Why don't you tell me what this is all about?" [49]

36. Comment on Gabe. Comment on situation. Foreshadowing her real reason for being there.

37. Gabe responds with his body to take control of the situation.

38. Addresses unease of tattoo. Empathy. Permission aspect of PLISSIT.

39. Continues to notice sexual aspects and wonders if she is reacting to him.

40. **C2: COMPLICATION/PLOT TURN**. Reveal. Action laced with emotion.

41. Emotional beat: metaphor.

42. Action response and body response. Intense familiarity.

43. Confirmation. This is Dana Parker.

44. Connection to Lorelei results in shaken emotional response.

45. Differentiation: Moderate emotion so judgment can be used.

46. Dismissive response from Dana. Deflects emotion.

47. Gabe challenges Dana with three pieces of information: Why not talk instead of read; sexually reacting (PEMS) to you; you've brought my past to the present. MICE. M: for their setting in C his history with Lorelei.

48. Dana confirms she knows him and addresses the sexual implications.

49. Back to the first line of story. Who is asking the question? Jerk, S&M junkie, or sucker for romance?

"Lorelei wanted to tell you herself. These are her words. You need to hear them from her, and then, well, we'll see. Please read the letter." [50]

Curiosity got the best of me. [51] Words from Lorelei. How could I not read the letter? Here was a chance for me to connect with her again. [52] In this tiny workspace, her presence felt larger than life. [53] I turned the envelope over in my hands, pondering what she had written. [54] Her talented hands had touched this, and now mine did. [55]

I noted the postmark; it was dated two months before she had died and a week after we had created the tattoos. [56] Dana stroked her arm in a nervous manner. Something about the movement caused me to wonder how soft her skin was, and if I would find out. Those things directed me dickward, again. *What the hell is it about this woman?* [57] I pulled the letter from the envelope and read. [58]

Hi Dana,

I hope this note finds you enjoying some fun European places. You work so hard on your photography. Your photos and stories will be famous and I remain your number one fan. [59]

What I am about to tell you has the potential to be a turning point in our lives. [60] *My search for a male soulmate has ended. I found him. His name is Gabe Stewart. Part of my heart now resides with this man.* [61] *He owns the most prestigious tat joint in the city. Besides being a hunk of a man who scares the crap out of most people and demands rough sex that is soooo good, he has a tender underbelly. Sex with him sends me into outer space. He is creative and soulful. He gives of himself, to all who matter to him, as if he has a limitless supply of heart.* [62]

50. Dana stands her ground through Lorelei to get what she wants.

51. Personality element.

52. Emotional intimacy with Lorelei.

53. Emotional beat: literary device.

54. Gabe holds the information, wondering what it is.

55. Physical connection to Lorelei through object and hands.

56. Sex history timeline: Gabe gathers info from postmark and places it on their relationship timeline.

57. Gabe's sexual connection with Dana.

58. Epistolary realism from Lorelei; a new POV.

59. Lorelei's connection to Dana established.

60. "Our lives" creates micro tension. Relationship reveal begins.

61. Male soulmate identified.

62. Description of Gabe, which has been demonstrated this far into story.

That offers me hope that he will accept you and me when I tell him about

us. [63]

He has no clue I go both ways, and I'm not sure what he will say. But baby,

I love you. I want our love to be joined with him. We can be family, I believe it.

After you get back from this current assignment, the introduction will happen and

we will work toward a great life together. You two are it for me. I want us to grow

old together in our sexual discovery and love. I refuse to think about it in any way

other than the three of us being together. [64]

I am sending you my kiss. I gave it to him, too. [65]

Loving you always and forever,

L.

Stunned and dazed, I looked up at Dana. Her intense eyes scrutinized me. I wondered how much

the emotion on her face mirrored mine. [66] The doorjamb barely supported my balance, but I

faltered again when she unzipped her jeans. [67] She put up a quick finger indicating for me to

wait a minute. I'm sure she saw a fool standing there with his mouth hanging open.

Taking her time, she pulled her jeans low over one hip and then slid her panties over. I

saw the tattoo. It was the same one that resided to the lower inside of my pelvic bone. My

reaction shattered me. This was insane. Getting my land legs under me, I moved a little closer

and bent over to look. Confirmed. That was our tattoo in the exact same location. [68] I blew out

a frustrated breath, as she yanked her clothes back together, not sure yet where to go with any of

this. [69] Attempting to get my wits together, I stuck my head out the door.

"Abraham." Dana jumped at my bark.

"Yeah, boss?"

63. Us. A full relationship reveal.

64. Lorelei wants polyamorous family. Point in sex history.

65. The tattoo connection of the three.

66. Emotion reflected both ways.

67. Response shifts. Which emotion runs it?

68. Tattoo identity confirmed.

69. Emotion: frustration. Differentiation employed.

"Close up the shop. We're done for the day."

"Boss, we still have appointments."

"Put a sign on the door saying we've had a family emergency and we will call to reschedule." [70]

"Yeah, you need anything?" He stuck his head in the room and scanned Dana, looking for a clue. She observed him, giving nothing away. [71]

"Probably, but not anything you can help me with."

"Ok. I'll take care of it. Call me if you need anything."

"Thanks, man. Will do."

It didn't take long for Abraham to escort everyone out. [72] The silence was louder than my heartbeat, and then Dana's voice pierced straight through it.

"Look, I'm fresh off a flight from Thailand. Do you have anything to eat or drink?" [73]

Good lord, she reminded me of Lorelei. Food and drink could be brought up in the middle of the most important conversations. I nodded my head.

"Yeah, I do. The stairs are this way."

I led the way down the hall and then we walked, side by side, up to my apartment. Her essence rocked between familiarity and newness. She was significantly shorter than Lorelei, whose head had met me just under my chin. With my more than six-foot stature, Dana hardly made it to my shoulder. [74] At the top of the stairs, a vision of Lorelei sitting in sheets in the middle of the bed popped into my mind. Remembering her words stopped me in my tracks.

"You think you know all about me, but you don't." [75]

70. Plan created.

71. Abraham checks to determine if Gabe is being a jerk, S&M junkie, or sucker for romance.

His connection to Gabe is a protector of Gabe hurting himself.

72. Plan executed.

73. Dana takes control.

74. Setting transition. Gabe contrasts Lorelei and Dana.

75. Gabe remembers Lorelei's words. Exposition. Sex history relationship timeline.

Dana cleared her throat, and I pointed toward the kitchen. At least for a bit, I would have something concrete to focus on.

"Omelet work?"

"God, that would be great. It's my favorite."

"Uh-huh."

I milled about getting the ingredients together. She refused coffee, but guzzled the cranberry juice and refilled the glass to go with her food. [76] Her full lips shimmered light red. I wanted to run my tongue across them to feel the texture and sample her taste with the cranberry juice. [77]

"Are you going to talk to me or play this gruff, silent type all night?" [78]

She had the most expressive mouth when she talked and ate. I wanted my lips on those lips, and her other lips.

Hell, what's stopping me? [79]

I strode over to the table and her eyes got big as she assessed my intent. Wrapping her long hair around my hand, I snatched her head back and inspected her face. Her breathing faltered. As I ran my finger along her jawline, the tension left her body. When those full, wet lips parted, I tasted her; she was sweet, tart, and warm. I sought out her tongue and sucked it hard. My sucking action pulled her to me, right out of that chair. I flattened my hand on the back of her head, securing her mouth to mine at the perfect angle so our bodies aligned. Dana wrapped her arms around my waist and her hard nipples rubbed across my chest. With a slight nip to her bottom lip, I pushed back. [80] "What took you so long?" [81]

Shock and confusion flitted across her face. "What?" [82]

76. Differentiation engaged. Focus on food activity.

77. PEMS desire. Physical. Micro-tension.

78. Question framed around Gabe's personality.

79. **C3: CRISIS**. Gabe is faced with a choice.

80. Set up for plot turn. Jerk? S&M junkie? Romance?

81. Plot turn.

82. Dana confronts the meaning of Gabe's words.

"You think you are the only one who got a letter? Frankly, after two years I had put you out of my mind, but Lorelei said you'd get here. And here you are. This what you expected?"

"Fuck, no." She dropped her arms.

"Yep, swears like a sailor. Definitely you."

"Fuck you." [83]

"We'll see. Maybe that and a lot more." [84]

Desire flew off her as I tossed her own words back at her. She was an easy read and liked my brazen personality. "It got the better of you, didn't it? You had to know what you were missing." [85]

That beautiful face and pouty mouth. She glared at me.

"What do you know?" I asked. [86]

"Lorelei told me everything. We could hash it all out, but I'm pretty certain it might be more satisfying to us both if you name what you want."

Dana plopped back into the chair at the kitchen table. She looked small and somewhat defeated. I squatted in front of her. I took both her hands in mine and looked up into that searching face. "Just tell me." [87]

"Okay. Okay. I want what you gave her. I want to feel what you made her feel. I want to feel alive again with sex." [88]

"That I can work with."

She gave my hands a squeeze. [89] "So you know, it was all her." She cocked her head like she was trying to get into mine. "She orchestrated, and she always fucked my brains out. You?"

83. Gabe responds in jerk mode and Dana meets him there.

84. Symmetry of Gabe using her words.

85. Gabe reads Dana's attraction and ties it to what he had with Lorelei.

86. Dana acquiesces to the feelings and situation.

87. Gabe changes emotion. Differentiation. Sets up opportunity for Dana to ask for what she wants.

88. **C3: CRISIS**. Faced with a choice, Dana names what she wants generically providing Limited Information to Gabe. (the LI in PLISSIT).

89. Gabe confirms Dana's request. Dana acknowledges confirmation.

"Yeah, she orchestrated all right, including now. Except now we get to decide what we do." [90]

"I'm a little concerned about that. Up until now I've only been with girls?" Disclosing that seemed to split her in half. And vulnerable looked good on her.

"Won't be a problem. I just come with the parts attached, not strapped on, and they're available for use. Exploring is exploring. I have wanted to explore you for a long time." [91]

"Me, too. And this attraction is real." A shadow or memory crossed her face. "You echo her words, you know." [92]

"I've had two years to consider this." I rubbed my thumb in the center of her palm, testing our connection. She reacted as if I'd pushed a start button in her hand. That was all it took.

"Okay, Gabe. Let's do this explore thing, but I want a shower first." [93]

Dana still had a questioning look, even in her declaration.

"Dana. I'm a sure thing. You will feel good."

"I'm counting on it. Which way to the shower?"

"This way. Let me get you a towel." [94]

As I ushered her to the bathroom and got her situated with supplies, I considered what I wanted to do. Hog-tying her came to my mind first. Dana had finally gotten here, and I wanted time with her. She showered fast, and the door opened, interrupting my thoughts. [95]

I turned. She stood naked, bold yet exposed.

She looked curvy with clothes; without them, she was a goddess. The long wavy hair had been tamed into a braid down one side of her head. Her chest rose as she took a deep breath and headed toward me. My dick strained against my pants, ready for action. [96]

90. Meaning of third person. Sex history.

91. Vulnerability met. The intimacy asked and acknowledged.

92. Dana acknowledges the place where Gabe and Lorelei intersect.

93. **C4: CLIMAX**. Decision made. Now the scene plays out with actions occurring based on decision.

94. Gabe reassures Dana. Romance.

95. Gabe centers himself and reflects on the past. Personality. Hog-tying. BDSM sex history.

96. PEMS. The view. Gabe's sexual body response.

She stopped a few feet from me. I wanted to give her some time, so I unbuttoned my shirt and observed her eyeing my muscles and my tattoos. She took two steps, placed her hands on my pecs, and pushed the shirt off my shoulders. The way she looked at me was as if she had discovered something for the first time. I wanted to be that discovery for her, for Lorelei. [97]

"I'd never been so interested in the male form sexually, Gabe. But you definitely have it going on." [98]

"Hop up here. Let's get some enjoyment going." She placed her thigh on my hip, and I palmed her ass and lifted her so we were face-to-face. As she grinned, her hot, wet pussy ground into me around my naval. [99] This skin-to-skin contact mirrored a spiritual experience. [100]

"You're all hard."

"In all the important places." She cocked her head, and leveled me with a gaze that made everything harder. [101] When her lips parted, my mouth and tongue went in for the kiss. The frenzy of her taste and her female warmth kicked me into a higher gear. [102] She climbed my body and the wet spot she trailed on my abdomen drove me insane. [103] I walked us over to the bed and dropped her on it. I had to get my jeans off for the total skin contact. [104]

She reclined on the bed in the most seductive manner. Her fingers danced across her tits and rubbed low in that lovely wet area of hers. She awaited the show. I unzipped my pants, and they hung on my hips for a minute as a mischievous quirk formed on her lips. *What must she be thinking?* [105]

"Stop right there, okay?" She scooted to the end of the bed and placed each foot on a thigh. Then she slid them north and found my erect penis. Her mouth rounded to an O shape. "This feels exciting like a new dildo in a strap-on." [106]

"It works just like one, too." Removing her feet, I dropped my pants to the floor.

184

97. Dana responds. Gabe's response is to let her lead because of her past and what he knew Lorelei would want.

98. Dana talks about Gabe's body in relation to her sex history.

99. Her dialogue prompts his moving things forward, to which she adds her own PEMS response. Gabe's Specific Suggestion (the SS in PLISSIT).

100. Gabe's internalization of the experience of her reaction to him.

101. Sex humor: hard and soft.

102. Gabe's urgent physical action. Reflecting on hard and soft. Kiss.

103. Dana's response matches Gabe's physical urgency.

104. Gabe matches Dana's physical response; wants more skin-to-skin (PEMS).

105. Dana's response to physical body change. New position with wonder and mischief.

106. Physical interaction and dialogue. Sex history. Motivation.

"It's bigger than what Lorelei used."

"We'll make sure it fits." [107] With her knees bent and her pussy glistening, I wasn't waiting any longer. It surprised her when I dragged her body to the edge of the bed and slurped my tongue through her juices. She wriggled around but my hands held her in place. I wouldn't let her move away. She was going to feel all that I had to give her. [108]

"Oh, my, God. Your tongue and your lips are blowing my mind. I have to taste me on you. Please, I need to kiss you." [109]

I nuzzled the tattoo lips on her hip with my nose before I kissed my way up her belly, stopping to worship both gorgeous breasts. Then we were nose to nose; my arms held my frame up over her. She grabbed my face and kissed me with searing heat. [110]

"It's so different."

She jockeyed for the dominant position, [111] but I intended to stay in charge, so I relaxed my weight on her so she would feel all of me. Soft curves and skin cushioned me. I was hot for her, but I rolled to my side. Lorelei had told me she was skittish. [112] With our legs entwined, my fingers trailed a path on her side, and I traced the tattoo lips at her pelvic bone. I marveled at how the heel of my hand fit into the hollow there. She squirmed, [113] the perfect mix of feisty and uncertain. Her photographer's eyes captured everything.

"If you could take a picture now that signified our predicament, what would it be?" [114]

"Oh, that's easy. I'd be sitting on your lap. My hand would be anchored on your tattooed hip, and we would be connected through the placement of your hand on mine."

"Sounds simple." [115]

"Well, no. There is more." She dropped her hand to feel my erection between us. She stroked me. I loved her tentative touch, and I ignited when it became more than tentative. [116]

107. Sex history dialogue.

108. Gabe's response to her sexual action is to give her what she asked for ("I want to feel what you made her feel").

109. Dana acknowledges PEMS; asks for specific activity (SS in PLISSIT).

110. Gabe physically transitions to that activity with his context.

111. Physical movement makes a statement out of Dana's exploration.

112. Gabe moves with want, but adapts, remembering sex history Lorelei shared.

113. Gabe creates the connection between past and present physically.

114. Gabe ties her behavior to her profession, giving her control with the question.

115. Gabe integrates the idea to the physical activity description and states his understanding.

116. Dana adds the sexual action element into the story.

"Show me."

"Okay, sit up and lean back on the pillows against the headboard. I'm going to grab my camera." [117]

I was sitting upright, penis included, when her naked form sashayed back in the room and placed the camera on the bed beside me. Her eyes focused on my manly part. [118]

"You are huge, you know. That girth is something else." [119]

Dana crawled up on the bed, straddled my lap with her knees on the bed, and rubbed her wet pussy all over my erection.

"I like how you feel, Gabe." She picked up the camera and snapped shots from the top angle. [120] My cock was sandwiched between us, helmet head bulging. Interest in photography left and insane desire arrived when she angled my penis down. She slathered her pussy juices all over me and rode me like a log. I sizzled. She took pictures of where our bodies met. I knew my cock would show up shiny and red. [121]

"You know I'm going in, right?" [122]

"I'm counting on it." [123]

I ran my fingers over the slickness on my cock, and as she pulled back, I used my fingers as if they were an extension of it to slide into her wet opening. [124]

"Oh, yes," I sighed and kept that rhythm as she groaned and clicked pictures. She could multitask with the best. The view was outstanding. She became a participant and an observer of our little party. [125]

"I want to snap the shot as you push that huge cock into me. Place your other hand here," she said. She took my hand and positioned it on her inked skin that intimately mirrored mine. "There." [126]

117. Gabe makes request and Dana responds.

118. Dana stays focused on the sexual element of the picture she is creating as a response.

119. Dana comments on Gabe's penis size. Reference to sex history.

120. Action to create picture. Sexual aspect. Sensation. Action Beat. Dialogue descriptor.

121. Seven sentences move the sexual action. Description. Sex focus. Feelings. Photography is now part of sex.

122. Gabe's sexual direction and plan.

123. Dana's confirmation of that plan. Consent.

124. Sexual action with fingers before cock.

125. Confirmation. Consent.

126. Dana gives direction. Verbal then physical. Desire. Motivation.

Her lips curled into a smile. Maybe I wasn't alone in feeling Lorelei's presence in the room. [127] "I'm going to put my hand by your tattoo. Tell me when you are going in, okay?" [128]

"Okay." I continued fingering her, and we had a hot mess of slickness between us. I was past ready to bury myself all up inside her. I rubbed circles around her clit, watching the intensity with which it stirred her rhythm. Then I felt it. She started to shake, and I knew she was on the brink. "Now," I moaned through gritted teeth. [129]

Dana arched her pelvis up to me as I pushed inside her; she ground her hand over my tattoo and her nails dug into my skin. We rocked together to the clicks of her camera work. At some point, she put the camera down, and I wrapped my arms around her body. I used my hands on her shoulders to drive her body down on my cock, over and over. Snaking my hand up, I grabbed her braid and yanked her head back, exposing her long neck. As my orgasm rushed through me, I created a mouth tattoo on her collarbone. Her body convulsed, and she moaned a tune until her orgasm subsided. [130]

I grabbed the camera and snapped her picture. Her talented lips, her exquisite neck outlined with the braid, and the long line of her body on mine. Proof that we captured pleasure. [131]

After I placed the camera on the pillow, she lazed around on top of me like an old dog getting comfortable in her spot. Skin thirst, that's what Lorelei used to call it. Well, Dana quenched mine. [132]

Curiosity must have gotten the best of her as she picked up the camera and examined her work. [133] In no time, I drifted into a post-orgasm coma. [134]

127. Gabe has a threesome reflection.

128. Dana confirms her plan, including the timing of insertion and photograph.

129. Micro tension. Clitoral stimulation and observation of body changes. Orgasm. Movement from Plateau phase into Orgasm phase.

130. Gabe has rush of emotion with physical intensity to reach orgasm. He notes her orgasm following his.

131. Physical action ties the overall story's meaning into the scene.

132. Gabe. Camera. Dana. PEMS. Skin thirst met. Action gives way to meaning of connection.

133. Dana looks at photos. Connection.

134. Gabe's sexual body response. Refractory period. Sleep.

When I awoke, Dana was gone. I should have hog-tied her. A note perched on the kitchen table. [135]

"Great omelet. Great sex. Great pictures. I swiped your cell number; I'll decide whether to use it." Her wary nature struck again. "She was right about you. Rough sex, tender underbelly. But hey, who needs another ink tattoo? You tattooed my lips forever." [136]

135. **C5: CONSEQUENCE.** Gabe's meaning and how the C4 CLIMAX affected the story.

136. **C5: CONSEQUENCE.** Dana's meaning.

Dr. J. 's Scenes-With-Sex Formula Example Forever Tattooed

DR. J.'S SCENES-WITH-SEX FORMULA

Character Sex History + Character's Needs/Wants + Character Connection
− Author Intrusion × Meaning of Sex = Type of Sex in Scene

Character Sex History
What sex event(s) from the character's past might be relevant to this scene?

Event:
P: G.gets tat. creates
E: connection between each other.
M: okay w/meaning
S: Rectified.

Event:
P: D. 1st FF experience.
E: A dare.
M: I'll try anything. want sex
S: meaning

Character's Needs/Wants
What does the character need and/or want at this moment?

They each want a relationship like they had with Lorelei.

Ease grief.

Find love.

Character Connection
(The Glue)
How is the character emotionally connected to the other character(s)?

Gabe & Dana connected by love or Lorelei and the dream she had for the three of them.

Author Intrusion
Which of your assumptions or biases might be drawn out by this scene?

How might a bisexual woman approach this situation? Different from a heterosexual women or lesbian?

Meaning of Sex
Why is the character having sex? What are they looking for?

For each of them to be close to Lorelei reaching for her yet creating new experiences that belongs to each of them.

Dana commented, " She orchestrate, and always fucked my brains out."

Gabe: "She orchestrated all right ... now we get to decide what we do."

Type of Sex in Scene
Considering all the factors above, describe the type of sex that makes sense for this scene.

Frenized. "It's finally here." Intense.

Each bold in different ways showing who they are.

Integrate the heart.

Work together as if making something.

It's like each person wants to reach into the other's skin to touch home and heart and Lorelei.

PLISSIT
Which sex-positive elements will influence this scene?

Permission:
Gabe tells Dana her feelings are normal.

Limited Information:
D. I've never been with a man. G. wants to explore her.

Specific Suggestions:
D asks for what she wants. Gabe for physical process.

The Fiction Writer's Sexuality Guide ©2024 | drjauthor.com

So, What's Left for You?

Pick up your purple highlighter and head to your manuscript.

Start at page one and read your entire document, highlighting any sexuality elements you've used in this book. This will give you a purple thread visual representation of how you have incorporated the sexuality elements from this book into your story.

Worksheets

Link: https://qr1.be/X9TE

Welcome to the full set of *The Fiction Writer's Sexuality Guide* Worksheets highlighted in the book. The first worksheet is Dr. J.'s Scenes-with-Sex Formula. It is to help you stay connected with holistic sexuality writing. Plug in information as you work each element within the book. You may see it as a composite of your total scene or story so keep your completed sheet close as you are writing.

For your convenience you can download a full set of fillable PDFs by scanning the QR Code above.

Where you start with the worksheets is up to you. Refer back to the example of the complete formula sheet in the book as needed.

Passion Works Community

If you would like kindred spirit authors to converse with about the book and worksheets, complete this Google Doc to be included in my private *Fiction Writer's Sexuality Guide* Group in the Passion Works Community on Discord.

Link: https://qr1.be/GIFQ

DR. J.'S SCENES-WITH-SEX FORMULA

**Character Sex History + Character's Needs/Wants + Character Connection
− Author Intrusion × Meaning of Sex = Type of Sex in Scene**

Character Sex History

What sex event(s) from the character's past might be relevant to this scene?

Event:	Event:
P:	P:
E:	E:
M:	M:
S:	S:

Character's Needs/Wants

What does the character need and/or want at this moment?

+

Character Connection
(The Glue)

How is the character emotionally connected to the other character(s)?

+

Author Intrusion

Which of your assumptions or biases might be drawn out by this scene?

−

Meaning of Sex

Why is the character having sex? What are they looking for?

✕

Type of Sex in Scene

Considering all the factors above, describe the type of sex that makes sense for this scene.

=

PLISSIT

Which sex-positive elements will influence this scene?

Permission:

Limited Information:

Specific Suggestions:

MY SEXUAL AWARENESS AND MINDSET

What are my attitudes about sex?

What topics might I be judgmental or dismissive about? Why?

Am I able to address, understand, and hold both sides of the sexuality coin?

Are my words inclusive of all people and behaviors?

How would I assess my attitudes toward sex in my writing?

ASSESSMENT OF SEXUAL HEALTH, PART 1

Elements of Sexuality

Name something you know or your character knows about the following elements of sexuality from the WHO's (2015) definition; then, name something you or your character would like to know more about.

Elements of Sexuality	I/They Already Know...	Would Like to Know More about...
Sex		
Gender identity and roles		
Sexual orientation		
Eroticism		
Pleasure		
Intimacy		
Reproduction		

How Sexuality is Experienced and Expressed

Identify how you or your character have experienced or expressed sexuality (WHO 2015).

Ways of Experiencing and Expressing Sexuality	Yes? Describe:	No?	Sort of? Describe:
Thoughts			
Fantasies			
Desires			
Beliefs			
Attitudes			
Values			
Behaviors			
Practices			
Roles			
Relationships			

ASSESSMENT OF SEXUAL HEALTH, PART 2

Influences on Sexuality

Describe how the following factors have influenced your or your character's sexuality (WHO 2015).

Factors	How This Has Influenced My or My Character's Sexuality
Biological	
Psychological	
Social	
Economic	
Political	
Cultural	
Legal	
Historical	
Religious	
Spiritual	

Assessment of Sexual Health

The following behaviors of sexually healthy adults are selected from "Life Behaviors of a Sexually Healthy Adult" on page 15 of *Guidelines for Comprehensive Sexuality Education* (SIECUS 2004): https://siecus.org/resources/the-guidelines/. Where are you/your character when it comes to these behaviors? Where do you/they want to be? Compare.

Behavior	Where I Am/Character Is	Where I/They Want to Be
Appreciate body		
Affirm gender identity and sexual orientation		
Develop and maintain meaningful relationships		
Avoid exploitative relationships		
Make informed choices about family options		
Live according to values		
Take responsibility for behavior		
Enjoy sexual feelings without needing to act		
Discriminate between helpful/harmful behavior		
Engage in honest, pleasurable, protected sex		

SEXUAL EVENT PEMS REFLECTION

Sexual Event

P: Physical

E: Emotional

M: Mental

S: Spiritual

Reflection
Thoughts? Feelings? New information gained?

CHARACTER PLANNING WITH SEXUALITY

Physical Description and Ability

Basic Information
(Name, age, pronouns, race, etc.)

Family

Culture and Ethnicity

Class and Education

Location and Region

Values and Ethics

Religion

Motivations and Desires

Emotions
(Honored? Dismissed? Regulated? Stereotyped?)

Personality

Mental State and Ability
(Neurodivergent? Trauma? Learning disability?)

Gender and Sexuality
Gender and sexuality can be influenced by all previous categories.
Has the character been positively or negatively influenced? Beliefs? Stereotypes?

SEX HISTORY INTERVIEW, PART 1

Learning about Sex: Overall

Answer the following questions on learning about sex overall for yourself or a character.

1 How did you learn about sex/sexuality? From whom? (For example, parents, caregivers, siblings, friends, school, media, internet, religion, spirituality)

_____

_____

2 What age were you?

_____

_____

3 What did you learn from parents or caregivers? Which subjects were covered? (For example, pregnancy, birth, intercourse, menstruation, nocturnal emission, masturbation)

_____

_____

4 Was the information accurate? What was your reaction? How did you feel?

_____

_____

_____

5 What did you learn from books, magazines, friends, or school?

_____

_____

_____

6 Was the information accurate? What was your reaction? How did you feel?

_____

_____

_____

7 What did you learn from personal experience?

_____

_____

_____

8 How did your culture, ethnicity, or family background influence your attitudes about sex/sexuality?

_____

_____

_____

9 What is the meaning/purpose of sex for you?

_____

_____

_____

SEX HISTORY INTERVIEW, PART 2

Learning about Specific Sexual Topics

Answer the following questions about specific sexual topics for yourself or a character.

1 Did you learn about sex from viewing or hearing a primal scene? What was your reaction?
_____
_____

2 What messages did you receive about masturbation and sex before marriage?
_____
_____

Family You Grew Up With

Answer the following questions about the family you or your character grew up with.

1 Were they sex positive, negative, or neutral?
_____
_____

2 What were the parents or caregivers' attitudes about sex? Degrees of openness?
_____
_____

3 What were the parents or caregivers' attitudes about nudity and modesty?
_____
_____
_____

4 What were sexual boundaries in your house? (For example, privacy, nakedness)
_____
_____
_____

5 How was affection demonstrated? Any incidences of discomfort to you?
_____
_____
_____

6 What were the messages about gender in your house?
_____
_____
_____

7 Were you caught or punished because of sexual activity?
_____
_____
_____

SEX HISTORY INTERVIEW, PART 3

Self

Answer the following questions about your or your character's individual experiences.

1 When did you realize your gender?

_____
_____
_____

2 When did you realize your attraction to others, or lack thereof?

_____
_____
_____

3 When did you start puberty? Describe your reaction.

_____
_____
_____

4 At what age did you discover masturbation? Describe your reaction.

_____
_____
_____

5 When was your first orgasm? Describe your reaction.

_____
_____
_____

6 At what age were you exposed to pornography? Describe your reaction.

_____
_____
_____

7 How were dating experiences in high school?

_____
_____
_____

Self, Continued

Answer the following questions about your or your character's individual experiences.

8 First sexual experience with another person? Different sex, same sex? Consensual, nonconsensual? Describe reaction.

_____
_____
_____

9 Have you experienced negative or upsetting sexual experiences? What effect has it had on you?

_____
_____
_____

10 How attractive do you feel (body image)? What factors contribute to this?

_____
_____
_____

11 How is sexual health overall? Physical health, STIs, concerns with sexual functioning?

_____
_____
_____

12 How do you feel about genitals? Yours? Your partner's?

_____
_____
_____

13 How often do you have sexual fantasies? Comfortable or uncomfortable with content?

_____
_____
_____

14 Have you ever had a sexual fetish?

_____
_____
_____

15 Is there anything about your sexuality or what/who you are attracted to that you are ashamed of? Who, what, when?

_____
_____
_____

OVERALL SEX HISTORY TIMELINE

Plot your or your character's sex history on the timeline below.
Place each event in the appropriate developmental stage.

Infancy
Birth to 18 Months
Trust vs. Mistrust

Early Childhood
Ages 2–3
Autonomy vs. Shame and Doubt

Preschool
Ages 3–5
Initiative vs. Guilt

School Age
Ages 6–11
Industry vs. Inferiority

Adolescence
Ages 12–18
Identity vs. Role Confusion

Young Adulthood
Ages 19–40
Intimacy vs. Isolation

Middle Adulthood
Ages 40–65
Generativity vs. Stagnation

Maturity
Age 65 and Onward
Ego Integrity vs. Despair

FOCUSED SEX HISTORY TIMELINE

Developmental Stage or Time Period: _____

Zoom in to a specific developmental stage or time period and plot the micro events within.
Consider how PEMS, PLISSIT, and the meaning of sex might be seen through the specific event.

EXPLORE TOP THREE SEXUAL FANTASIES

Reflection on Lehmiller's (2020) Study, Part 1

Describe sexual fantasies you and your character have had within Lehmiller's top three categories.

Group Sex (You)

Group Sex (Character)

BDSM (You)

BDSM (Character)

Novelty, Variety, Adventure (You)

Novelty, Variety, Adventure (Character)

How could you integrate sexual fantasy into your story while avoiding author intrusion?

EXPLORE SEXUAL FANTASIES

Reflection on Lehmiller's (2020) Study, Part 2

Describe sexual fantasies you or your character have had beyond Lehmiller's top three.

Sexual Fantasy: _____

Sexual Fantasy: _____

Sexual Fantasy: _____

Sexual Fantasy: _____

How could you integrate these sexual fantasies into your story while avoiding author intrusion?

THE CYCLE OF SELF: MODEL

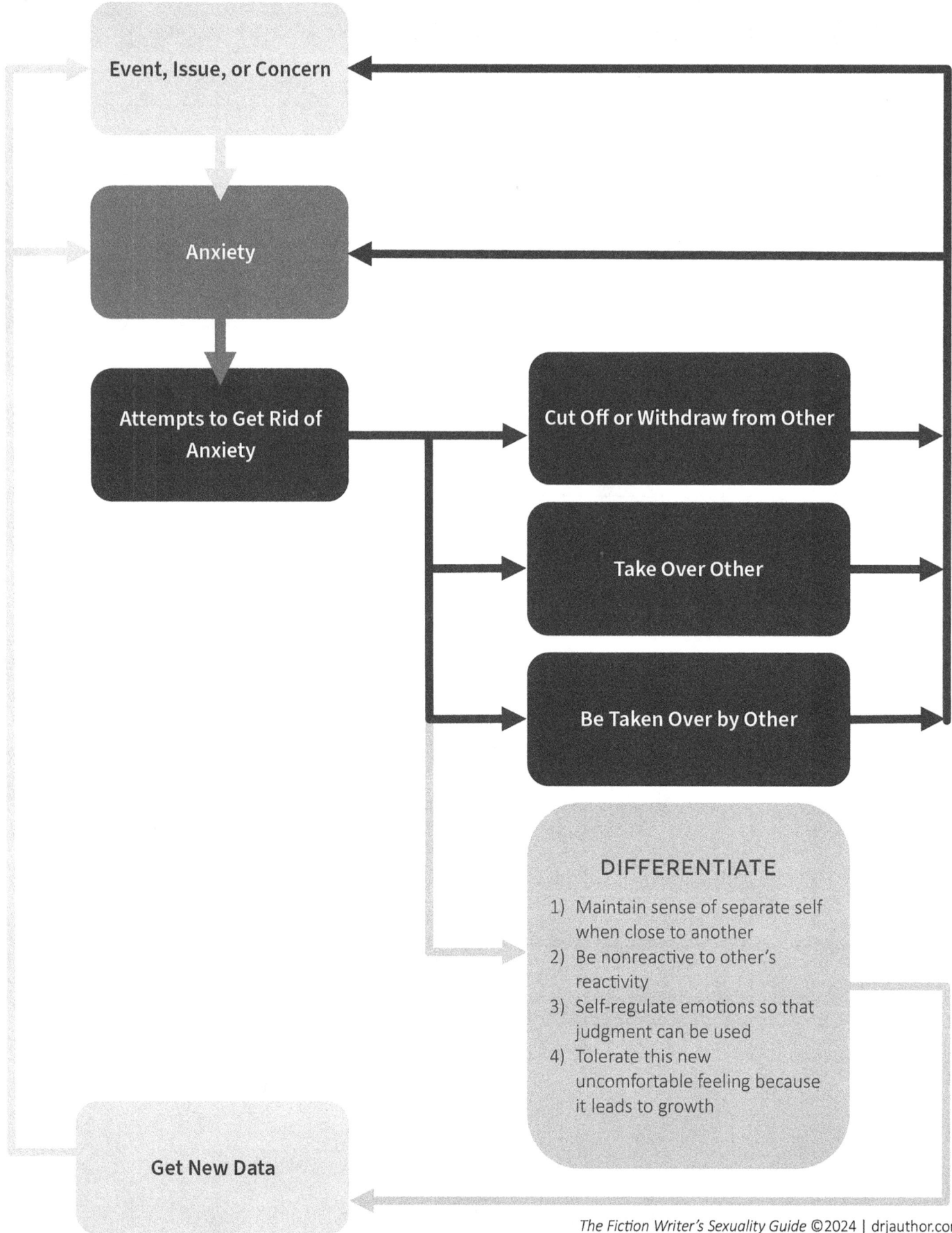

Event, Issue, or Concern

Anxiety

Attempts to Get Rid of Anxiety

Cut Off or Withdraw from Other

Take Over Other

Be Taken Over by Other

DIFFERENTIATE

1) Maintain sense of separate self when close to another
2) Be nonreactive to other's reactivity
3) Self-regulate emotions so that judgment can be used
4) Tolerate this new uncomfortable feeling because it leads to growth

Get New Data

The Fiction Writer's Sexuality Guide ©2024 | drjauthor.com

THE CYCLE OF SELF: PRACTICE

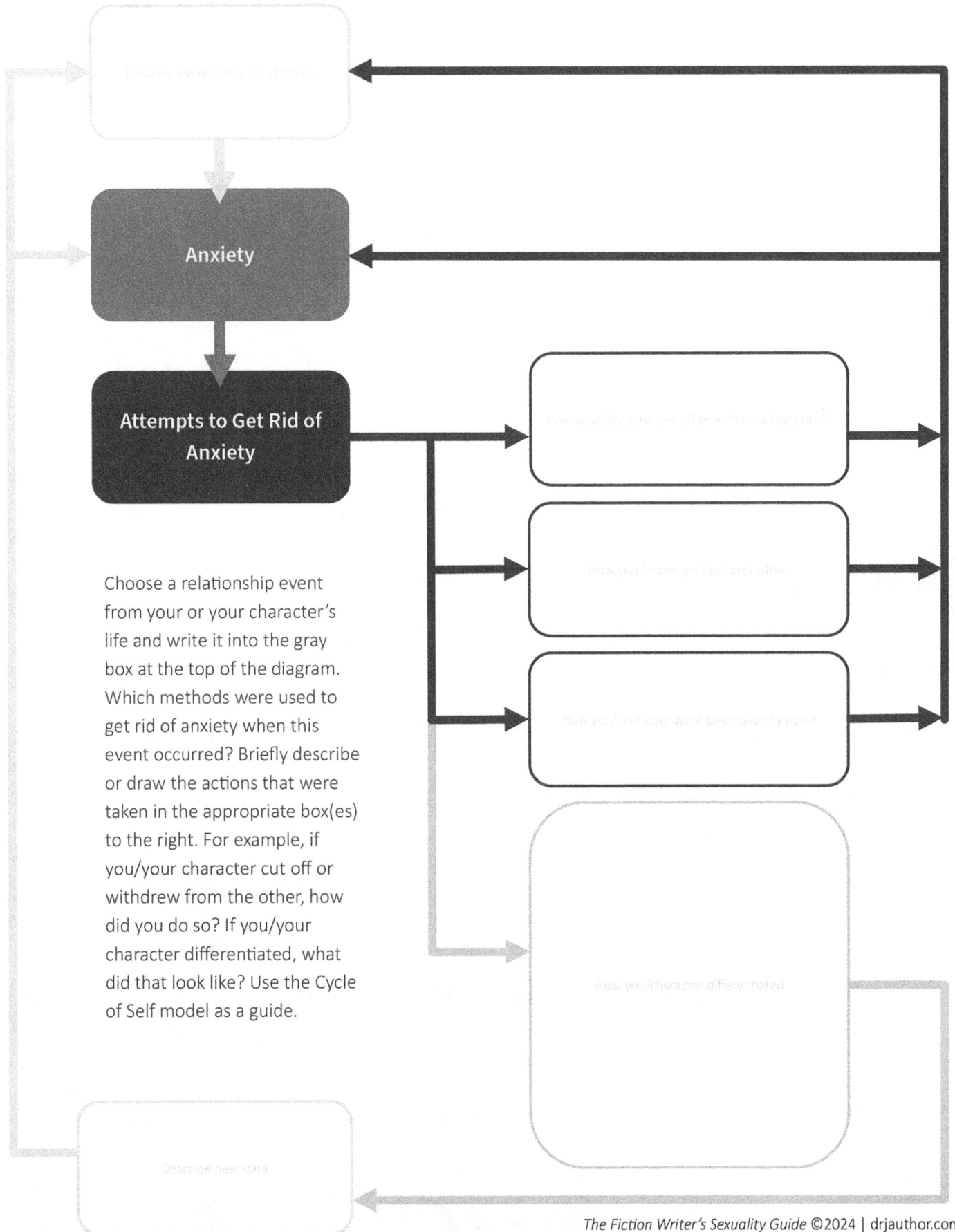

Choose a relationship event from your or your character's life and write it into the gray box at the top of the diagram. Which methods were used to get rid of anxiety when this event occurred? Briefly describe or draw the actions that were taken in the appropriate box(es) to the right. For example, if you/your character cut off or withdrew from the other, how did you do so? If you/your character differentiated, what did that look like? Use the Cycle of Self model as a guide.

Anxiety

Attempts to Get Rid of Anxiety

EXPLORE A NONMONOGAMOUS CHARACTER

Part 1: Motivations

Describe the type of consensual nonmonogamy your character engages in.

Check "Y" if the motivation (Lehmiller 2021) factors into the character's choice to be nonmonogamous; check "N" if it doesn't. Then use the remaining column to identify where the motivation originated in the character's history.

Motivations	Y	N	Origin of Motivation
Autonomy			
Belief Systems			
Relationality			
Sexuality			
Growth and Expansion			
Pragmatism			

Part 2: Day-to-Day

How does your character negotiate with their partners to make the relationships work?

How does your character handle jealousy and other difficulties that come with CNM?

FISHER'S PERSONALITY FITS: CHARACTER 1

Start by circling the personality type (Fisher, n.d.) that best suits your character,
then explore the ways your character embodies that personality type.

Explorer	Builder	Director	Negotiator

Positives
Strengths of this personality type?

Negatives
Weaknesses of this personality type?

Words
Words you associate with this character's personality?

Jobs
Professions this character is drawn to?

Partners
Kinds of partners this character is drawn to?

Connection
Ways of connecting this character prefers?

FISHER'S PERSONALITY FITS: CHARACTER 2

Start by circling the personality type (Fisher, n.d.) that best suits your character,
then explore the ways your character embodies that personality type.

| Explorer | Builder | Director | Negotiator |

Positives
Strengths of this personality type?

Negatives
Weaknesses of this personality type?

Words
Words you associate with this character's personality?

Jobs
Professions this character is drawn to?

Partners
Kinds of partners this character is drawn to?

Connection
Ways of connecting this character prefers?

FISHER'S PERSONALITY FITS: COUPLE

First, summarize significant points from the two previous character sheets. Then use the side-by-side visual to highlight items that could create tension as well as opportunities for real connection between your characters.

Character Name: _____

Personality Type: _____

Character Name: _____

Personality Type: _____

How Does Your Couple Mesh?

Compile main areas for building tension and connection from the two individual character sheets.

STORYTELLING AND NEUROCHEMISTRY

Questions on "Empathy, Neurochemistry, and the Dramatic Arc" by Paul Zak (2013)

What emotions were elicited?

1. _____

2. _____

What is different about the story of Ben and his father going to the zoo?

_____
_____
_____
_____
_____
_____
_____
_____
_____
_____

What chemical was produced for each?

1. _____

2. _____

What does each chemical do?

1. _____

2. _____

What does the research tell us about storytelling?

_____
_____
_____
_____
_____
_____
_____
_____
_____
_____

What were the brain activity areas for the emotional story of Ben and his dad?

1. _____

2. _____

SCIENCE OF STORYTELLING

Questions on "The Magical Science of Storytelling" by David JP Phillips (2017)

What is the significance of the eBay story?

What is the significance of the Bond story?

What core element caused people to buy something in both stories?

What does Phillips use the story about falling in love to show?

What is the "angel's cocktail"?

What is the "devil's cocktail"?

EXPLORE PLAY IN SEX

Describe how you could incorporate the following types of play into sex—your own or your character's.

Ritual Play

Rough-and-Tumble Play

Imaginative Play

Body Play

Object Play

PLAN YOUR SCENE TYPE

Number (Who)
Who will be in the scene? How many?

Action (What)
What is happening? Anything unexpected?

Surroundings (When, Where)
Indoors or outdoors? Time/date/season?

Variety
Have you used this scene type before?

Tension (Why)
How will the tension of this scene push the character(s) to a dilemma during which they must make a choice?

SEXUALITY AT THE SCENE LEVEL

Describe how the following sexuality concepts will apply to the specific scene you're constructing.

The Holistic Nature of the Character

PEMS and Sex Positivity

PLISSIT

Eliminating Author Intrusion While Being Informed by Author Emotions

Brain Science of Storytelling, Play, and Sex

Character's Sex History, Personality, and Differentiation of Self

MICE

Macro, Micro, Mezzo: How Does Your Overall Story Arc Inform This Scene?

THE 5 CS OF SCENE

Create a scene or select a written scene and identify the components of Heather Whitaker's 5 Cs.

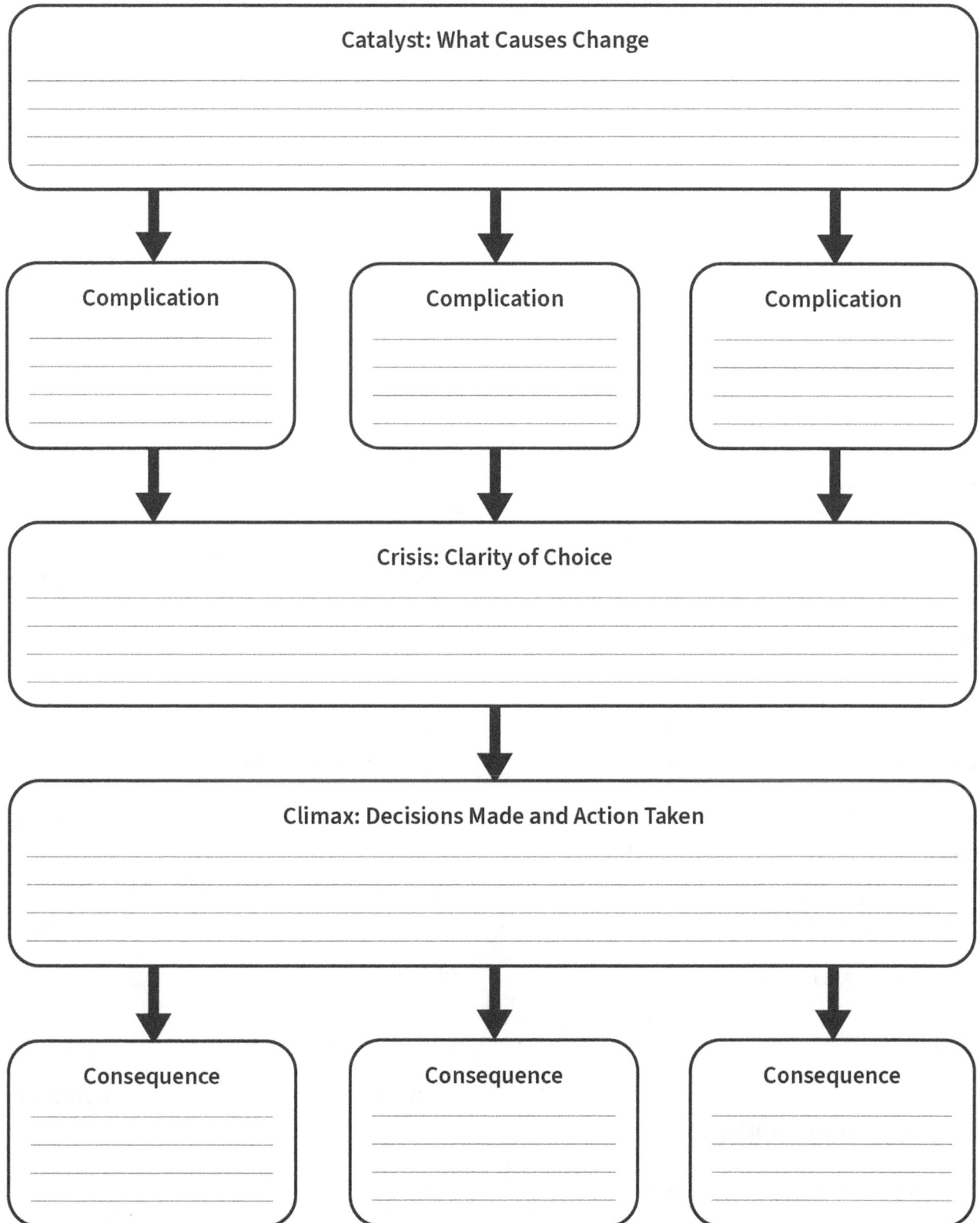

Catalyst: What Causes Change

_____
_____
_____
_____

Complication

_____
_____
_____

Complication

_____
_____
_____

Complication

_____
_____
_____

Crisis: Clarity of Choice

_____
_____
_____
_____

Climax: Decisions Made and Action Taken

_____
_____
_____
_____

Consequence

_____
_____
_____

Consequence

_____
_____
_____

Consequence

_____
_____
_____

SCENE CONSTRUCTION CHECKLIST

Use this checklist to help you navigate the parts of your scene—or scenes you read from other authors. You may discover areas you want to refine. Use this information to help you create a bank of examples; they will help you learn and grow in your writing.

Opening

☐ Was I pulled into the POV character's situation Immediately?

Character

☐ Did I get a sense of their identity?

☐ Did I get a sense of their wants and needs?

☐ Could I "see" them to some degree?

☐ Did their emotion come through?

Plot

☐ Did I understand what was happening?

☐ Were characters working toward individual goals?

☐ Did the storyline keep me interested?

Setting

☐ Did I feel like a part of the scene?

☐ Details? (Enough, too little, too much?)

Dialogue

☐ Did I know who was speaking?

☐ Enough dialogue? (Or too little, too much?)

Pacing

☐ Did the scene flow well? (Or too slow, too fast?)

☐ Was I able to follow the events as they happened?

Description

☐ Could I see what was happening clearly?

☐ Strong imagery used?

☐ Did I skim, or feel distracted as I read?

☐ Was it interesting?

☐ Was more detail needed to make the scene feel more important or real?

Voice

☐ Was the writing unique in some way?

☐ Did I feel like only this writer could write this story?

☐ Did the viewpoint feel authentic?

Ending

☐ Did it feel complete?

☐ Did the scene end on a cliffhanger or create the urge to read on?

PRACTICE THE SEXUAL EMOTIONAL BEATS

Choose a scene with sex that features two characters. Select a sentence of dialogue spoken by one, then write the other's reaction in ten different ways, using a different emotional beat each time (Cowley 2014).

Starting Sentence

_____

_____

Emotional Beat Responses

1 Internal physical sensation:

_____

2 External physical sensation:

_____

3 Physical action:

_____

4 State the emotion:

_____

5 Use something distinctive to your character or story world:

_____

6 Setting:

_____

7 Metaphor or simile:

_____

8 Mini flashback:

_____

9 Mini flashforward:

_____

10 Surreal imagery:

_____

Sexual Menu Du Jour

Special of the Day

Cocktails

Appetizers

Main Course

Sides

Dessert

Outside the Bedroom

What happens before physical activity?
Brainstorm in the outer gray area.

Inside the Bedroom

Describe physical activities. Use arrows to show what
the "outside the bedroom" activities develop into.

Resources

- American Association of Sexuality Educators, Counselors, and Therapists (AASECT): https://www.aasect.org/referral-directory.

- Brian McNaught: https://www.brian-mcnaught.com/.

- Helen Fisher: https://helenfisher.com/.

- *How to Build a Sex Room*: https://www.imdb.com/title/tt21030224/.

- *The Language of Lust, Love, Sex*: http://www.sex-lexis.com/.

- To learn more about *How I Learned to Drive*, visit the play's Wikipedia page: https://en.wikipedia.org/wiki/How_I_Learned_to_Drive.

- From the Psychology Group Fort Lauderdale: "20 Questions to Assess Your Hidden Gender Biases and How They Harm the LGBTQ+ Community." https://thepsychologygroup.com/how-hidden-gender-biases-harm-the-lgbtq-community/.

Abbreviations

BDSM. Bondage and Discipline, Dominance/submission, Sadism and Masochism.

5 Cs of Scene. Catalyst, Complications, Crisis, Climax, Consequences.

CNM. Consensual Nomonogamy.

MICE. Milieu, Idea, Character, Event.

PEMS. Physical, Emotional, Mental, Spiritual.

PinV Intercourse. Penis-in-Vagina Intercourse.

PLISSIT. Permission, Limited Information, Specific Suggestions, Intensive Therapy.

POV. Point of View.

SIECUS. Sex ed for social change.

STIs. Sexually Transmitted Infections.

References

Annon, Jack. 1976. "The PLISSIT Model: A Proposed Conceptual Scheme for the Behavioural
Treatment of Sexual Problems." *Journal of Sex Education and Therapy* 2 (1): 1–15.
https://doi.org/10.1080/01614576.1976.11074483.

Aponte, Harry J. 2016. *Person of the Therapist Training Model.* London: Taylor & Francis
Group.

Archer, Jodie, and Matthew Lee Jockers. 2016. *The Bestseller Code: Anatomy of the Blockbuster
Novel.* New York: St. Martin's Press.

Brockington, Guilherme, Ana Paula Gomes Moreira, Maria Stephani Buso, Sérgio Gomes
228irs.228a, Edgar Altszyler, Ronald Fischer, and Jorge Moll. 2021. "Storytelling
Increases Oxytocin and Positive Emotions and Decreases Cortisol and Pain in
Hospitalized Children." *Proceedings of the National Academy of Sciences* 118 (22).
https://doi.org/10.1073/pnas.2018409118.

Balfe, Caitríona, Sam Heughan, Sophia Skelton, and Richard Rankin. 2020. "Why The Cast Of
'Outlander' Never Reads Ahead." Interviewed by Maril Davis. *Around the Table,*
Entertainment Weekly, March 2, 2020. https://www.youtube.com/watch?v=xgNJBa-
1hUs.

Biga, Lindsay M., Sierra Dawson, Amy Harwell, Robin Hopkins, Joel Kaufmann, Mike
LeMaster, Philip Matern, Katie Morrison-Graham, Devon Quick, and Jon Runyeon.
2019. "27.5 Physiology of Arousal and Orgasm." *Open.oregonstate.education,*
September.

"Biology of Female Sexual Function» Sexual Medicine» BUMC." N.d. www.bumc.bu.edu.
Accessed January 7, 2024.

https://www.bumc.bu.edu/sexualmedicine/physicianinformation/biology-of-female-sexual-

function/#:~:text=Following%20sexual%20stimulation%2C%20neurogenic%20and.

Bowen, Murray. 1978. *Family Therapy in Clinical Practice.* New York: Jason Aronson.

Brown, Stuart. 2008. "Play is More Than Just Fun." Filmed May 2008 by Serious Play at Art

Center Design Conference, Pasadena, CA. Curated by TED.com.

https://www.ted.com/talks/stuart_brown_play_is_more_than_just_fun/.

Burke, Tammy. 2023. "Our Brains on Story." MyStoryDoctor.com. June 15, 2023.

https://mystorydoctor.com/our-brains-on-story/.

Card, Orson Scott. 1999. *Elements of Fiction Writing: Characters and Viewpoint.* Cincinnati:

Writer's Digest Books.

Chatham, Wes and Ty Franck. 2022. "Wes Chatham & Ty Franck of 'The Expanse' Discuss the

Show's Finale and Future." Interviewed by Jon Weigell. Rolling Stone, January 11, 2022.

Audio, 7:20. https://www.youtube.com/watch?v=lk0ekQacgs8.

Cowley, Katherine. 2014. "Writing Powerful Emotion Beats in Fiction." Blog. June 24, 2014.

https://www.katherinecowley.com/blog/writing-powerful-emotion-beats-in-fiction/.

Creative, My, Business Goals For 2022 With Joanna Penn, and The Creative Penn says. 2021.

"Story or Die with Lisa Cron." Www.thecreativepenn.com. December 13, 2021.

https://www.thecreativepenn.com/2021/12/13/story-or-die/.

Cron, Lisa. 2012. *Wired for Story: The Writer's Guide to Using Brain Science to Hook Readers

from the Very First Sentence.* Berkeley: Ten Speed Press.

Deshmukh, Vishwajit, Bharat Sontakke, Kirubhanand, Gayatri Muthiyan, Patil, Akanksha Dani,

Austin Psychiatry, and Behav Sci. n.d. "The Enigma of the Sexual Brain: A

Comprehensive Review of Neurobiological Perspectives." Accessed January 7, 2024. https://austinpublishinggroup.com/psychiatry-behavioral-sciences/fulltext/ajpbs-v9-id1093.pdf.

Dictionary.com. s.v. "language." Accessed October 24, 2023. https://www.dictionary.com/browse/language.

Dictionary.com. s.v. "sensual." Accessed October 24, 2023. https://www.dictionary.com/browse/sensual.

Dr. J. [pseud.] 2022. "Create a Play Practice in Sex—Your Brain Will Thank You." *XOXO Blog*, Rosy Wellness, Inc. July 2022. https://meetrosy.com/blog.

Dr. J. [pseud.] 2017. "Infused Leather." In *Best Women's Erotica, Volume 3*, edited by Rachel Kramer Bussel, 222-230. Jersey City: Cleis Press.

Fisher, Helen. N.d. "Personality." Accessed October 24, 2023. https://helenfisher.com/personality/.

Fisher, Helen and Lucy Brown. N.d. "Welcome to the Anatomy of Love." Accessed October 24, 2023. https://theanatomyoflove.com/.

Foerster, Anna and Ronald D. Moore, 230irs. 2014. *Outlander*, Season 1 Episode 7: "The Wedding." Aired September 20, 2014, on Starz. https://www.netflix.com/title/70285581.

Friedman, Edwin. 1990. *Friedman's Fables*. New York: Guilford.

Gabaldon, Diana. 2016. *"I Give You My Body…": How I Write Sex Scenes*. Canada: Double Day.

"Guys on the 'Side': Looking beyond Gay Tops and Bottoms." 2013. HuffPost. April 16, 2013. https://www.huffpost.com/entry/guys-on-the-side-looking-beyond-gay-tops-and-bottoms_b_3082484.

Grisham, John. 2018. "Shrouded in Mystery: John Grisham on His New Novel, 'The Reckoning.'" Interview by Norah O'Donnell and Gayle King. *CBS This Morning*, CBS News, October 23, 2018. 3:48–4:33. https://www.youtube.com/watch?v=FkUyakxQFcU.

Humm, Philipp. 2023. "Storytelling and the Brain: The Neuroscience behind Stories." Power of Storytelling. February 7, 2023. https://power-of-storytelling.com/storyscience/.

James, E. L. 2015. *Fifty Shades of Grey*. London: Arrow Books.

Kelly, Brian and Ronald D. Moore, 231irs. 2014. *Outlander*, Season 1 Episode 6: "The Garrison Commander." Aired September 13, 2014, on Starz. https://www.netflix.com/title/70285581.

Kinkly. 2019. "Cisgender." Janalta Interactive, October 14, 2019. https://www.kinkly.com/definition/922/cisgender.

Kinsey Institute. 2022. "Polyamory and Consensual Non-monogamy in the US." *Kinsey Institute Research & Institute News*, June 6, 2022. https://blogs.iu.edu/kinseyinstitute/2022/06/17/polyamory-and-consensual-non-monogamy-in-the-us/.

Kleinplatz, Peggy J., and A. Dana Menard. 2020. *Magnificent Sex: Lessons from Extraordinary Lovers*. New York: Routledge.

Lehmiller, Justin J. 2021. "6 Reasons People Want Consensually Nonmonogamous Relationships." *Sex and Psychology* (blog). May 31, 2021. https://www.sexandpsychology.com/blog/2021/5/31/6-reasons-people-want-consensually-nonmonogamous-relationships/.

Lehmiller, Justin J. 2020. *Tell Me What You Want: The Science of Sexual Desire and How It Can Help You Improve Your Sex Life*. New York: Da Capo Press.

Lehmiller, Justin J. 2018. *The Psychology of Human Sexuality.* Hoboken: Wiley Blackwell.

Lehmiller, Justin J. 2019. "What Does It Mean To Be Sex Positive." *Sex and Psychology* (blog).

October 9, 2019. https://www.sexandpsychology.com/blog/2019/10/9/what-does-it-

mean-to-be-sex-positive/.

McKinney, Kristin. n.d. "The Effects of Adrenaline on Arousal and Attraction."

Www.mckendree.edu.

https://www.mckendree.edu/academics/scholars/issue17/mckinney.htm.

Mcleod, Saul. 2023. "Erik Erikson's stages of psychosocial development." *Simply Psychology.*

October 16, 2023. www.simplypsychology.org/Erik-Erikson.html.

Oxford University Press. s.v. "heteronormative." Accessed August 29, 2023.

https://www.google.com (search "heteronormative").

Phillips, David JP. 2017. "The Magical Science of Storytelling." Filmed March 16, 2017 at

TEDxStockholm, Stockholm, Sweden. https://www.youtube.com/watch?v=Nj-

hdQMa3uA.

"Play and the Feel Good Hormones." n.d. Primal Play. https://www.primalplay.com/blog/play-

and-the-feel-good-hormones#:~:text=being%20more%20alive.-.

Robinson, Lawrence. n.d. "The Benefits of Play for Adults - HelpGuide.org."

Https://Www.helpguide.org. https://www.helpguide.org/articles/mental-health/benefits-

of-play-for-adults.htm#:~:text=While%20play%20is%20crucial%20for.

Schnarch, David Morris. 1991. *Constructing the Sexual Crucible: An Integration of Sexual and*

Marital Therapy. New York: Norton.

Schnarch, David Morris. [1993] "Hugging 'til Relaxed." Clinical training presented at David

Schnarch, San Diego, California.

Sexuality Information and Education Council of the United States (SIECUS). 2004. "Life

    Behaviors of a Sexually Healthy Adult." In *Guidelines for Comprehensive Sexuality*

    Education, 3rd ed., 15. Fulton. https://siecus.org/resources/the-guidelines/.

Silverman, George. 2022. "Mindskills 101." *The Mind Skills Playbook*, revised December 25,

    2022. https://publish.obsidian.md/mindskills-

    playbook/_MindSkills+Playbook/Mindskills+101.

Vangralova, Zhana. [2021] "Open Smarter." Course taught through www.drzhana.com/open-

    smarter.

Watts, Leslie, Valerie Francis, Anne Hawley, and Kim Kessler. n.d. "Editor Roundtable:

    Brooklyn." *Editor Roundtable*, Story Grid. https://storygrid.com/editor-roundtable-

    Brooklyn/.

Whitaker, Heather. 2017. "Grand Unified Theory of Writing." Course presented at Heather

    Whitaker, Tallahassee, Florida

World Health Organization (WHO). n.d. "Sexual Health." Accessed October 24, 2023.

    https://www.who.int/health-topics/sexual-health#tab=tab_2.

World Health Organization (WHO). 2015. *Sexual Health, Human Rights and the Law*. Human

    Reproduction Programme. July 2015.

    https://www.who.int/publications/i/item/9789241564984.

Zak, Paul. 2013. "Empathy, Neurochemistry, and the Dramatic Arc." *The Future of Storytelling*,

    YouTube. Feb 19, 2013.

    https://www.youtube.com/watch?v=DHeqQAKHh3M#action=share.

Index